Jesse James

Legends of the Wild West

Sitting Bull

Billy the Kid

Calamity Jane

Buffalo Bill Cody

Crazy Horse

Davy Crockett

Wyatt Earp

Geronimo

Wild Bill Hickok

Jesse James

Nat Love

Annie Oakley

Legends of the Wild West

Jesse James

Adam Woog

CHELSEA HOUSE
PUBLISHERS
An imprint of Infobase Publishing

Jesse James

Copyright © 2010 by Infobase Publishing

Chelsea House
An imprint of Infobase Publishing
132 West 31st Street
New York NY 10001

Library of Congress Cataloging-in-Publication Data
Woog, Adam, 1953-
 Jesse James / Adam Woog.
    p. cm. — (Legends of the wild West)
 Includes bibliographical references and index.
 ISBN 978-1-60413-598-5 (hardcover)
 1. James, Jesse, 1847–1882—Juvenile literature. 2. Outlaws—West (U.S.)—
Biography—Juvenile literature. 3. Frontier and pioneer life—West (U.S.)—Juvenile
literature. 4. West (U.S.)—History—1860-1890—Juvenile literature. 5. West (U.S.)—
Biography—Juvenile literature. I. Title.
 F594.J25W66 2010
 364.15'52092—dc22
 [B]   2009036993

You can find Chelsea House on the World Wide Web at
http://www.chelseahouse.com

Text design by Kerry Casey
Cover design by Keith Trego
Composition by EJB Publishing Services
Cover printed by Bang Printing, Brainerd, Minn.
Book printed and bound by Bang Printing, Brainerd, Minn.
Date printed: February, 2010
Printed in the United States of America

10 9 8 7 6 5 4 3 2 1

This book is printed on acid-free paper.

All links and Web addresses were checked and verified to be correct at the time of publication. Because of the dynamic nature of the Web, some addresses and links may have changed since publication and may no longer be valid.

CONTENTS

THE OUTLAW JESSE JAMES

History still remembers many of the daring bandits and killers who lived in the Old West. Billy the Kid, Butch Cassidy and the Sundance Kid, and Belle Starr are just four who gained fame during that wide-open era. But the most celebrated outlaw of them all, growing more legendary with every passing year, is Jesse James. In *Desperate Men: The James Gang and the Wild Bunch*, historian James D. Horan comments, "Jesse James is one of our cherished folklore legends and nothing seems to diminish our perennial interest in him."

There are several reasons for this continued fascination. For one, James's escapades symbolize the anything-goes thrills of the Old West. His canny strategy to target banks and trains—a bold new idea at the time—caught the public's imagination. And his larger-than-life personality was exciting—especially when stories about him were heavily embellished, as they always were. Historian T.J. Stiles, in *Jesse James: Last Rebel of the Civil War*, comments, "His is a tale of ambushes, gun battles, and daring raids, of narrow escapes, betrayals, and revenge."

Although he was accused of committing horrible crimes, Jesse James was a popular figure and celebrity due to his daring escapes that put his name in the newspapers. After his death in 1882, James became an even greater legend, bearing the controversial image of a heroic outlaw.

HIS PLACE IN HISTORY

Jesse James's reputation was that of an American Robin Hood. According to legend, he stole from the rich and gave to the poor, protecting small farmers from ruin.

The outlaw's defiant image also had a political side. A proud son of Missouri, James was active in the years after the Civil War when tensions remained high between Northern and Southern states. The South's crushing defeat by the Union led to lasting resentments. James and other Confederate (Southern) loyalists swore revenge.

The band that Jesse and his brother Frank led with another set of brothers, the Youngers, allegedly targeted banks and train lines owned by Northern businessmen. In his many letters to newspapers, James bragged that his crimes represented a defiance of the hated Union. Others, however, saw—and still see—James and his gang differently. To them, the bandits were little more than ruthless criminals concerned mostly with their own welfare. These opposing views have led to decades of debate over his role in American history. Horan comments:

> With each new robbery or murder [Southerners] would insist that 'the Boys' were only misguided champions of the Confederacy who had been driven into a life of banditry by the war. But [Northerners] would loudly declare that the Jameses and Youngers were nothing but common thieves and murderers who should be hanged [from] the nearest tree.

Good or bad, much of the Jesse James legend is wrong, or at least questionable. There is no doubt that he was a killer: James murdered at least 12 people, and he claimed the number was 17. Nor is there doubt that he was successful at robbing dozens of banks and trains and making and spending fortunes. And he did manage to avoid capture, proving unstoppable until a traitor shot him.

On the other hand, there is scant evidence that James's true motive for his crimes was political revenge or to right social injustice. Southerners primarily owned the banks he robbed, and, for the most part, these targets were in the South. Most of the people he and his gang killed were Southerners, as were the lawmen and politicians who hunted the outlaws. Furthermore, the robberies often affected ordinary people more than the rich, because it was their savings that were taken. Unlike today, no federal protection for bank deposits existed then.

Finally, it seems that James and his gang rarely, if ever, gave to the poor. Evidence indicates that they kept the loot for themselves and spent the money they stole. The many stories about James's charity toward those less fortunate were probably invented. Historian Robert Barr Smith writes, "My view is that the James boys and the Younger brothers were no more than ordinary criminals, bullies who stole the fruits of others' labors because it beat working and did a good deal to inflate their twisted egos."

Was Jesse James a hero or a villain? It is impossible to choose one or the other, because there is a little truth on each side of the debate. In *Jesse James Was His Name*, historian William A. Settle Jr. comments, "Badman or Robin Hood—take your choice! Whichever form of the legend you favor, both are based in fact."

JESSE JAMES IS BORN

The future legend, Jesse Woodson James, was born on September 5, 1847. His birthplace was his family's farm in Clay County, Missouri, near Centerville (the present-day town of Kearney). The baby was named for his mother's brother, Jesse Richard Cole, and his father's brother, Drury Woodson James.

Jesse's father, Robert S. James, was a Baptist preacher and farmer from Kentucky. He was a well-educated man, proud of his extensive personal library. According to a newspaper of the time, Robert was "well known in this community . . . and a man much liked by all" for his gentle good nature.

Zerelda James Samuel was born in 1825 in Woodford County, Kentucky. After losing her father when she was a small child, she was raised by her grandfather, who owned a saloon. Later she became a Confederate sympathizer and strongly defended the activities of her boys Frank and Jesse.

Jesse's mother, Zerelda E. Cole James, was different. Like her husband, she was a native of Kentucky, but she was also tough-minded, with a hot temper and a commanding manner. A relative once commented, "Zerelda had always given orders, but she had never taken any. . . . The mother of Frank and Jesse James was strong-willed and had plenty of determination."

The couple met when Robert was a ministerial student, and they married in 1842. He was in his early twenties, and Zerelda was even younger. Writer Homer Croy comments in *Jesse James Was My Neighbor*, "She was only sixteen, a minor, and Robert James . . . didn't have enough worldly goods to indicate he could support her. So he had to put up a bond of fifty pounds of tobacco in order, as the documents say, 'to intermarry' Zerelda E. Cole."

CHANGING FORTUNES

The newlyweds traveled to Missouri, where Zerelda's mother lived, and decided to settle there. Things went well for the family at first. Robert helped start the New Hope Baptist Church and a Baptist school, William Jewell College, in Centerville. He also owned and managed a 245-acre (99-hectare) farm. This work was necessary to the couple's survival because in those days Baptist congregations did not pay their preachers.

The Jameses soon had three children: Alexander Franklin, called Frank, born in 1843; Jesse; and Susan Lavenia, born in 1849. Two others, Robert B. and Mary, died in infancy.

Unfortunately, the Jameses' luck changed in 1849. Robert James decided to travel west alone. He wanted to be part of the stampede of people who headed out to seek their fortunes in the California Gold Rush that year. There has been much speculation as to why Robert left his family. He may simply have sought wealth, as did so many others. He may have wanted to preach among the California miners. Or he may simply have been eager to get away from Zerelda. By all accounts, she was difficult to live with, given to scolding her husband and objecting to his habit of leaving for long periods to preach in small Missouri towns.

Robert's trip to California was difficult, and it took three months to reach his destination. Once he got there, his stay was brief. Only a few weeks after arriving, he died in a town called Hangtown (now Placerville), probably from an infection of some kind. Even simple infections could be common causes of death in the days before the invention of antibiotics.

REMARRIAGE

Zerelda was suddenly the single parent of three young children, and this put her in serious financial straits. Robert had left considerable debt. He had no will, so all of his possessions went to the children. A local man was appointed to represent Frank, Jesse, and Susan. Many of the family's belongings, including the contents of their farmhouse and their livestock, were then auctioned off to settle their debts. A collection taken up by Robert James's church helped a little. Still, it was a desperate situation.

Zerelda felt she had little recourse but to marry again. She wed a farmer named Benjamin Simms, who was almost twice her age and very wealthy. Simms and the children disliked each other, so the James kids were sent to stay with another family. It must have been a confusing and frightening time for Jesse, who was only five.

The marriage soon soured. Zerelda later remarked that it failed because she was unwilling to be apart from her children for long. Zerelda and Simms separated, and before their divorce was finalized, Simms died in a fall from a horse.

A THIRD MARRIAGE

Zerelda then married a mild mannered doctor, Reuben Samuel, in September 1855. (Some sources spell his name Samuels.) The strong-willed Zerelda found it easy to dominate her quiet new husband. He moved in with the James family and, probably in accordance with his new wife's wishes, gave up medicine to tend to their farm.

The children liked Samuel and called him Pappy. In time, four more children—Jesse's half-brothers and sisters—were born. They were Sarah Louisa (also called Sarah Ellen), John Thomas, Fannie Quantrell, and Archie Peyton. According to some sources, the outgoing Jesse was the dominant child among this brood. Beyond that, the James and Samuel kids tended to be the leaders of the children from surrounding farms.

They attended the local schoolhouse, Pleasant Grove School. Jesse only finished fifth grade and had no interest in education, in contrast to his older brother. Frank enjoyed exploring his late father's library, especially the works of William Shakespeare. Reportedly, Frank had his eye on becoming a teacher.

When not in school, the children were busy with chores around the farm, such as plowing, harvesting corn, and taking care of the family's horses. Robert Barr Smith comments that the James kids grew up "used to the good things of Missouri farm life: lots of hard work, a close family, and church on Sundays."

GROWING INTO MANHOOD

The older boys spent much of their free time hunting game and riding horses. Guns were standard equipment in virtually every household in the Old West, so Frank and Jesse learned to use shotguns and pistols at an early age. They also learned to ride. Horses and horse-drawn wagons and carriages were the main means of transportation.

Jesse grew to be a handsome teenager. He was about five feet seven inches (170 centimeters) tall with light brown hair, a slender build, and a high, broad forehead. Later in life, Jesse often sported whiskers. He had blue eyes, which he blinked frequently. Historians think this was caused by a chronic inflammation called granulated eyelids.

Beyond all this general information, few details are known about Jesse James's early life. After he became famous, many biographies and "dime novels" about him added more. (Dime novels, also called "penny dreadfuls," were very popular but often inaccurate stories. They had thrilling titles like *Jesse James' Narrow Escape, or Ensnared by a Woman Detective*.)

Jesse was no different from other boys on the American frontier of the mid-nineteenth century. Besides working on the family farm, he cared for the horses and learned to hunt. He used his knowledge of guns later during the border wars.

Some of these books tried to picture Jesse and Frank as being cruel and ruthless even from childhood. There is no confirmation of such claims, however, and it is likely that they were invented to make the stories more exciting. Settle writes, "There is no evidence to show that Frank and Jesse were any better or any worse than normal boys of their time and circumstance."

A WAR SHAPES JESSE'S LIFE

As Jesse grew into adulthood, one historic event above all had a profound impact on how he would think and live for the rest of his life. Around the time he was 14 years old, the division between North and South led to the Civil War, a split largely created by the issue of slavery. Slavery had cataclysmic and far-reaching effects on society as a whole, but it also intensely influenced individuals like the James boys. Settle writes, "Through [the] accident of time and place of their birth, Frank and Jesse entered life in the midst of great events in the making."

These events were responsible, in large part, for Jesse's career in crime. The Civil War instilled in the young man a profound hatred of the North and a fierce loyalty to the South. These feelings prompted Jesse to become a guerrilla fighter during the war.

After the South's defeat, he turned his experience as a fighter to the world of crime, claiming that he did so for revenge. The James boys' lives were thus deeply intertwined with the issues of the Civil War. In *The Saga of Jesse James*, writer Carl W. Breihan comments, "Anyone hoping to understand the circumstances surrounding the lives of the Jameses must undertake a careful study of pre-Civil War days and the period of Reconstruction [after the war]."

ON THE BORDER

Missouri, Jesse's home state, lay between the antislavery North (also known as the Union) and the proslavery South. When states in the South decided to secede and form their own nation, the Confederate States of America, it was primarily so that slavery could continue there. Missouri, a border state (a slave state that bordered a state that prohibited slavery), was itself split. Some parts were sympathetic to the Union side, others to the Confederacy, and it could not firmly commit itself to either.

The population of Jesse's native Clay County was generally pro-South. In fact, it was nicknamed "Little Dixie," after the popular name of the Deep South. Clay County, not surprisingly, was also strongly in favor of slavery. Slaves accounted for about one-quarter of the state's population when Jesse was born.

Furthermore, the county bordered Kansas, which was not yet a state. In 1854, Congress had passed the Kansas-Nebraska Act. This created the Kansas and Nebraska territories and gave their citizens the right to determine the issue of slavery within the territories. Many homesteaders in Kansas were in favor of abolishing slavery.

Missourians in Clay County and elsewhere on the Kansas border wanted slavery for Kansas. They feared, among other things, that their property would be in danger with a free state so close at hand. Historian Roger A. Bruns, in *The Bandit Kings: From Jesse James to Pretty Boy Floyd*, writes, "[T]he delicate balance between the supporters and opponents of slavery [was] violently shaken by the passage of the Kansas-Nebraska Act." In a preview of the bloody war to come, the Kansas-Missouri border saw numerous lynchings, rigged elections, guerrilla violence, and burned farms.

THE FAMILY AND SLAVERY

Along with their neighbors, the combined James-Samuel family was firmly in the proslavery camp. Robert, Jesse's father, had owned six slaves, and the 1860 census records showed that Reuben Samuel had seven.

These slaves were essential to the family's prosperity and ability to work a large farm. Stiles notes that they "were [Zerelda's] most valuable property. . . . [T]hrough both the headline-grabbing [proslavery] struggle and pure self-interest, a Southern identity rooted itself firmly in her household."

Thus, slavery was the norm in Jesse's world as he grew up. Nearly everyone around him approved of the practice, and by the time he became a teenager it was an explosive issue. Northerners and Northern sympathizers were hated villains who sought to destroy a treasured way of life. Jesse James was thoroughly caught up in this conflict.

THE
WAR YEARS

When the Civil War began in 1861, Missouri—caught between the North and the South—was hit hard. Union forces imposed martial law that year, and many pro-Confederacy Missourians were forced to move from the state. Violence and destruction were rampant. Some Union soldiers felt free to plunder or destroy whatever they could. Bands of antislavery guerrilla fighters from Kansas, called jayhawkers, often crossed the border to raid Missouri.

Missouri had its own guerrilla fighters, called bushwhackers. The bushwhackers, also known as home guards or militiamen, had no official connection to the Confederate Army, but they did everything they could to disrupt any pro-Northern sympathizers in the state. T.J. Stiles writes, "Secessionist bands struck across the state, destroying railroad tracks, tearing down telegraph wires, burning bridges, sniping at Federal sentries, and terrorizing loyal families."

The growing culture of violence had an obvious effect on young men like Jesse James. Roger A. Bruns notes, "[A] whole generation of tough, teenage boys on the Kansas-Missouri border grew up brandishing guns and knives and anticipating armed conflict at any moment."

With the passing of the Kansas-Nebraska Act, guerrilla groups on both sides of the slavery issue viciously attacked citizens in Kansas and Missouri. Frank joined one of the proslavery groups, Quantrill's Raiders. Jesse also tried to join but was considered too young. In this depiction, the Raiders destroy buildings and terrorize citizens in Lawrence, Kansas, in 1863.

QUANTRILL'S RAIDERS

As the war dragged on, bushwhackers continued to wage a miniature version of the larger conflict. They had an advantage over Union troops and jayhawkers who did not know the countryside well. The bushwhackers could travel and hide with relative ease across the state's rugged territory.

Support from a majority of Missouri's residents gave them further protection. As William A. Settle Jr. points out, "Guerrilla fighting behind enemy lines cannot be carried on successfully without a sympathetic civil population to sustain it with shelter, subsistence, information, and men."

Frank James was the first of the brothers to enlist in this small-scale warfare, probably in 1862. He joined a company of bushwhackers that was a part of the Missouri State Guard and fought with them in at least one battle until he fell ill and had to return home.

After his recovery, Frank continued the fight in a succession of other bands. The most notable of these was the famous Quantrill's Raiders. Its leader, William C. Quantrill, was a Southern loyalist who became a bushwhacker because he hated the discipline of the regular army.

Quantrill became a major problem for the Union forces occupying Missouri. One Union captain, W.S. Oliver, wrote, "I have seen this infamous scoundrel rob mails, steal the coaches and horses, and commit other similar outrages upon society even within sight of this city [Independence]. Mounted on the best horses in the country, he has defied pursuit."

LOADING AMMUNITION

Legend has it that the teenage Jesse also rode with Quantrill, but this has never been proven. It seems likely that the group's leaders thought he was still too young. They apparently did make use of Jesse by putting him to work loading revolvers.

The Lawrence Massacre

Although it has never been proven, some sources say that both Jesse and Frank James took part in bushwhacker William C. Quantrill's most notorious raid: the massacre in August 1863 of some 200 men and boys in Lawrence, Kansas. The aim of this well-planned mission was to kill any men in the town who might be pro-Union.

Historian T.J. Stiles writes, "They shot every man and boy they saw. They pulled them out of cellars and attics, knocked them off horses, and executed them in front of their families. They clubbed them, knifed them, stole their money and valuables, burned their homes and businesses."

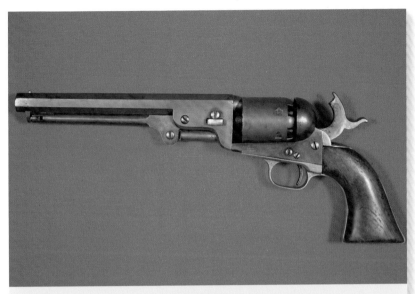

Pictured is a model of a .36 caliber Colt revolver. Because he was too young to be a fighting member of Quantrill's Raiders, Jesse contributed by reloading revolvers for the guerrilla group. It is said that Jesse lost the top of his middle finger from an accident while loading guns for the Raiders.

This was a tedious and time-consuming job but an important one. The bullets and guns that the bushwhackers used were not sophisticated. The bushwackers favored old-fashioned .36 caliber Colt Navy revolvers. Each of the gun's six chambers had to be filled with gunpowder and a lead ball. This was rammed home and sealed with grease, after which a percussion cap was fitted on each chamber.

These guns were difficult to load or reload even in the best of circumstances, and impossible in the heat of a fight. As a result, bushwhackers routinely carried five or six revolvers each in their belts, pulling new ones out as needed to avoid having to reload. They also often had rifles or shotguns.

Loading revolvers was not just tedious, it was dangerous as well. For most of his life, Jesse James was missing the tip of one middle finger. According to some accounts, the injury was the result of an accident while loading guns.

RAID ON THE JAMES-SAMUEL FARM

In 1863, midway through the war, a group of Union soldiers raided the James-Samuel farm. Jesse and his mother had been under surveillance for some time because they were suspected of carrying messages to and from bushwhackers. The Northerners' main purpose, though, was to find Frank and other members of his band.

The soldiers briefly hanged Reuben Samuel from a tree, trying either to kill him or to torture him. In either case, Jesse's stepfather was eventually cut down; he survived, although he bore rope marks around his neck for years.

According to some accounts, the soldiers also beat Jesse. Still, they did not succeed in learning Frank's whereabouts from the family. They only succeeded in intensifying Jesse's determination to fight them.

Sometime in 1863 or 1864, Jesse was finally allowed to join a group of guerrilla fighters. He was not a professional soldier, but a terrorist targeting people who, in different times, might have been friendly neighbors. Stiles writes, "[T]his, then, was his introduction to warfare; not as a gladiator in battle against a tyrannous foe, but as a member of a death squad, picking off neighbors one by one."

JESSE BECOMES A BUSHWHACKER

Jesse got his first taste of combat in May 1863. He, Frank, and about a dozen others raided Richfield, Missouri, a town that had some citizens who were sympathetic to the North. A man named Fletch Taylor led this group of bushwhackers, but Jesse soon joined another band under the command of William T. Anderson.

Even in a world of brutal men, "Bloody Bill" Anderson and his gang were particularly vicious. Bruns writes, "For Missouri Confederates, killing . . . was a patriotic thing, and in Bill Anderson's bunch, butchery was encouraged." They were in the habit, for instance, of hanging the scalps of their victims from their saddles. (Union soldiers were also known to practice scalping.)

Anderson was not shy about his intentions. He made this clear in an open letter to the newspapers of Lexington, Kentucky, warning its citizens, "I will hunt you down like wolves and murder you. You cannot escape." On another occasion, Bloody Bill pinned a note on a victim that referred to one of his lieutenants, Archie Clement: "You come to hunt bush whackers. Now you are skelpt. Clemyent skept [sic] you. Wm. Anderson."

Although slight and still baby-faced, Jesse proved himself capable of being part of this bloody world. He soon became an admired and trustworthy member of Anderson's gang. The leader reportedly once stated, "For a beardless boy, he is the best fighter in the command."

JESSE IS WOUNDED

Anderson's gang became increasingly dangerous to the military units of the North assigned to occupy Missouri. On numerous occasions, the Union forces tried to track the bushwhackers down. On one mission, a contingent of Union soldiers was sent out from Plattsburg, Missouri. Jesse's mother notified him and the rest of Anderson's group by messenger of this turn of events.

The depleted forces in Plattsburg left the Union fort there vulnerable. Anderson's band was able to storm in and capture a supply of guns, ammunition, and money. The North retaliated, among other ways, by exiling the James-Samuel family—minus Jesse and Frank, who disappeared—to Nebraska until the end of the war.

In August 1864, Jesse received his first serious wound, although it was not in battle. A farmer shot Jesse in the chest as he tried to steal a saddle from a fence. The bullet passed clean through Jesse's torso, missing his vital organs, but it was still a dangerous injury.

The gang took Jesse away, and a doctor treated him in the home of a Confederate sympathizer. He recovered quickly. After only a month of recuperation, the young outlaw was able to rejoin Anderson's gang.

In 1864, Missouri was full of militia groups and mayhem. At the age of 16, Jesse (*shown above*) joined a particularly brutal group of bushwhackers, led by William "Bloody Bill" Anderson. Jesse became, as Anderson stated, "the best fighter in the command."

THE CENTRALIA MASSACRE

That September, Anderson and about 80 others set fire to a train and burned the depot in Centralia, Missouri. The bushwhackers also captured and killed 24 unarmed Union soldiers stationed there.

The massacre led to a large-scale battle. It was a victory for the bushwhackers, who lost only a handful of men while killing 123 out of 155 Union soldiers. Frank James later claimed that his brother fired the shot that killed the Union commander of the battle, but this cannot be verified. Although Frank was definitely at the Centralia battle, there is no hard evidence that Jesse was there.

A month later, Bloody Bill Anderson—who had been personally responsible for at least 50 deaths—was killed in an ambush. Bloody Bill's death effectively dissolved his band of guerrillas. Stiles comments, "[T]he changes wrought by . . . Anderson's demise were inescapable. The old band was breaking up, as small clusters of men drifted off, each taking its own direction, and the James brothers drifted off as well."

Frank rejoined Quantrill and headed to Kentucky with him. Meanwhile, under the command of Archie Clement, Jesse and several others went south for the winter to either Texas or Mexico (the sources differ). The brothers both returned home in the spring of 1865, as the war was drawing to a close.

IN AN AWFUL FIX

The Civil War officially ended that April. In Appomattox, Virginia, the leader of the Confederate Army, General Robert E. Lee, formally surrendered to his Union counterpart, General Ulysses S. Grant. Small pockets of the Confederate Army, scattered across the South, also surrendered as they received word of the war's end.

There are several conflicting stories about Jesse and Frank James during this period. According to one told in later years by Jesse, he and Frank traveled to Lexington, Missouri, where they planned to surrender to Union major J.B. Rogers. Jesse claimed that he was leading the way, carrying a white flag of surrender, when his group encountered a troop of drunken Union soldiers. The soldiers fired without warning on the bushwhackers. It may also have been that the guerrillas happened to stumble into an army patrol that was able to fire first.

In any case, the guerrillas returned fire and scattered. During the skirmish, Jesse was again shot in the chest. This time, a .36 caliber bullet from a Navy revolver seriously wounded a lung.

Still, Jesse managed to escape and take refuge. He later stated, "I was near a creek, and I lay in the water all night—I felt as if I was burning up. The next morning, I crawled up the bank and there was a man plowing nearby who helped me get to my friends. . . . I was in an awful fix [and] everybody thought the wound would be mortal."

As with so much of James's history, accounts of the incident differ. One version has him making his way on his own to see his family. In another version, he surrendered but was so close to death that the commanding Union officer, Major Rogers, did not bother making Jesse take the oath of allegiance normally required of surrendering Confederates. Rogers stated that he believed the bushwhacker "would soon be surrendering to a higher authority."

In this account, Rogers ordered that the dying man be given use of a wagon, a driver, a little money, and a pass to visit his family. Jesse's mother and stepfather were in Rulo, Nebraska, just across the Missouri River from their home state.

However it happened, Jesse did join his family in Nebraska at least through the summer of 1865. But the wounded outlaw, fearing that he was close to death, said he wanted to die on Missouri soil. He was transported by a horse-drawn carriage to his uncle's boarding-house in Harlem, Missouri.

RECOVERING

During Jesse's stay in Harlem, his first cousin, Zerelda "Zee" Mimms, tended to him. She changed his dressings, brought him food, and cooled his fever. In those days before antibiotics, serious wounds such as those from gunshots took a long time to heal, but the young man did begin to recover slowly. A friend later wrote about him, "In the spring of 1866 he was just barely able to mount a horse."

According to the James family, it was several years before Jesse was fully recovered. Some historians, however, have questioned the seriousness of Jesse's injury. Evidence indicates that he was able to ride fairly soon after being shot. Stiles writes, "In truth, Jesse James's multiyear recuperation was a retroactive alibi, manufactured after he had become famous to hide his activities in the years immediately following the war's end."

Meanwhile, members of the James-Samuel family began to return to their home in Kearney. Frank came back from Kentucky, where he had continued raiding with Quantrill's band even after the Confederate surrender. Along with the family came a few former slaves who had once belonged to them. They accompanied the family, Stiles notes, "perhaps out of loyalty, perhaps because [they] could realistically imagine no other future than a continued life of labor on this farm."

CHAOS ACROSS THE SOUTH

During this period, the United States was still in turmoil from the ravages of the long war. At least 620,000 soldiers had died in the conflict, both Union and Confederate, as well as thousands of civilians. In this and other ways, the entire nation had been deeply affected by the war, but the states of the defeated Confederacy were hit the hardest. All across the South, there was ample evidence of devastation and death. Although not officially part of the Confederacy, Missouri had suffered, too. A third of its citizens had been killed or driven from their homes. Bridges, levees, and other necessary structures were gone. The economy had collapsed into near-ruin. Farms, livestock, and even entire villages had been destroyed. Robert Barr Smith comments, "All of western Missouri was scarred by stone chimneys standing alone and forlorn, like headstones, above the charred ruins of burned-out homes."

It was a bleak time for the conquered Confederates. As the North asserted its hold on the South, many people on both sides tried to take the law in their own hands. James D. Horan comments that, as a result, power in the region often came from the barrel of a gun: "Law was the Colt strapped around a man's waist." This, then, was the atmosphere to which Jesse returned after recovering from his wound.

LIFE AFTER THE WAR

Missouri's political structure was also in chaos during the postwar years. This period after the Civil War was called Reconstruction because the North worked to build the South up, by restoring what had been destroyed and by implementing new political and social changes.

Large numbers of Confederate sympathizers remained in Missouri, but a new, Northern-backed government controlled the state's politics. Similar conditions existed in other states of the South as well. This government enacted many sweeping changes. For example, it passed a state constitution that freed all slaves, echoing what the Emancipation Proclamation and the Thirteenth Amendment did on a national level. Also, former Confederates were held responsible for any acts they committed during the war, whether they were soldiers or civilians, while Northern soldiers were granted full amnesty from prosecution for many crimes.

Furthermore, all men in Missouri were required to take an oath that they would commit no acts of rebellion. Confederate sympathizers who refused to sign could not vote, hold public office, become a deacon of a church, serve on a jury, or even work in certain professions such as doctor or businessman. Carl W. Breihan writes

The Civil War had devastating effects on the entire nation, but the South was hit especially hard. The period after the war was called the Reconstruction Era (1865–1877), when the North led an effort to rebuild the South and establish order. This painting shows an optimistic view of developments in the South during Reconstruction in 1867.

that such laws had the effect of "condemning them to menial labor or forcing them to leave the state."

HE WAS LIKED BY EVERYONE

In short, the postwar period was a volatile and uncertain time. As might be expected, much of the South felt humiliated by its defeat and outraged at the new laws, which were considered harsh and vindictive. Violence still flared up, sometimes between individuals but often involving bands of bushwhackers who swore continued revenge against the North. Union troops were also on edge and sometimes attacked Southerners.

The bushwhackers' pledges to continue the violence were as true for the James boys as they were for other outlaws. Breihan comments, "As far as Frank and Jesse James were concerned, the war had not really ended where actual hostilities were concerned." They continued to wage their own small-scale battles.

In May 1865, Archie Clement's group, which included Jesse, rode into Clement's home territory, Johnson County, Missouri. There they carried out several massacres, including one in which the bushwhackers attacked the town of Kingsville, burning houses and killing eight men and boys as they stumbled out of bed. According to legend, Jesse shot and killed the town's postmaster.

When not out on raids, Jesse spent most of his time at the family home. It appears that his life there was very different from his other life. He made it seem as if he had given up his violent ways, joining a Baptist church and becoming a regular member of the community. According to a family friend, Dr. W.H. Ridge, Jesse was "quiet, affable, and gentle in his actions. He was liked by everyone who knew him."

Not everyone who knew Jesse had similar views. One local merchant, Daniel Conway, commented that Jesse "has been leading a wandering, reckless life . . . and ever since the war has been regarded as a dangerous and desperate man."

THE JAMES BOYS BECOME ROBBERS

Jesse's quiet home life did not last long. When Archie Clement put a new gang together, Jesse joined it. Nevertheless, the times were changing. As the North solidified its hold on the South, it maintained increasingly firmer control over the bushwhackers. Continued guerrilla warfare against the Union forces began to seem futile.

Largely because of this, Clement's band added a new twist to their activities: robbery. Besides attacking Union sympathizers and soldiers, the band—and other gangs of bushwhackers—also began robbing banks.

These roving groups of fighters had lost their old reason for existence, but they found a new purpose as they transformed themselves into bands of criminals. Author William Settle Jr. comments, "Former guerrillas found a new outlet for their unruly natures—bank robbing. In all probability, boredom and the inability to adjust to the calm of postwar life drove them to crime, though their defenders assert that they were avenging wrongs inflicted by rapacious [greedy] bankers."

A HISTORIC ROBBERY

Bank robbery was not a new idea. In fact, the first recorded bank robbery in the United States occurred in 1798, when the nation was little more than two decades old. Other robberies continued sporadically in the years after that.

The first documented bank robbery during the Civil War occurred in October 1864, when a group of Confederate outlaws traveled from Canada into the United States. They took over St. Albans, Vermont, and boldly declared that the town was now in the possession of the Confederate States. Then the gang looted every bank on the town's main street and made off with a fortune. One source estimated it at $200,000—well over $2 million in today's money—though this figure was probably inflated.

Although this adventure was successful, bank robbery was not yet an art. The nation had not seen an organized gang carry out a regular, systematic series of holdups. It appears that Archie Clement's group was the first to do so. Its first job—the first armed bank robbery in the United States after the war—took place in February 1866.

On this occasion, Clement and his boys held up the Clay County Savings Association in Liberty, Missouri. According to some sources, Clement specifically targeted the bank because its owners were former antislavery militia officers.

On the appointed day, the bandits stationed themselves around the town square. It was early in the morning, and passersby did not pay much attention when two strangers, both wearing the kind of overcoats common among soldiers, entered the bank. The other robbers (some reports estimated a dozen) stayed outside to stand guard.

The bank's cashier, Greenup Bird, was alone in the bank except for his son, William, who also worked there. (In those days, a bank cashier was an important person in the business, more or less equivalent to a manager.) The two strangers asked to change a $10 bill. When William Bird started to make change, both men produced revolvers and jumped over the counter.

The bandits ordered them to open the vault and threatened to kill both if they made any noise. Greenup Bird later commented, "I hesitated and began to parley [negotiate]," he recalled. "He told me that if I did not go in instantly [to the vault] he would shoot me down. I went in."

Inside the vault, the two men produced a cloth sack of the sort commonly used to hold cotton or wheat. The Birds were instructed to fill it with money, both paper and gold coins. The robbers then shoved the Birds in the vault and closed it. The vault door was not locked, however, and as soon as they could, the father and son ran outside to raise the alarm.

They were too late. The robbers were riding quickly away, having collected a reported $58,000—roughly $761,000 in today's money. There was one casualty during the robbery, and it was accidental. A bystander, a student at William Jewell College, was killed when one of the robbers' horses kicked him during the escape.

Two large groups were quickly formed to track down the robbers. They tracked the gang as far as a spot on the Missouri River opposite Sibley. They lost the trail at that point, however, probably because the bandits rode their horses into the river to cover their tracks.

AN UNSUCCESSFUL SEARCH

It has never been proven that Jesse and Frank James took part in this robbery. It is likely, however, since they were regular members of the Clement gang by this time. If there is uncertainty about the James boys' participation in the Clay County Savings robbery, there is no doubt that they had a hand in later holdups.

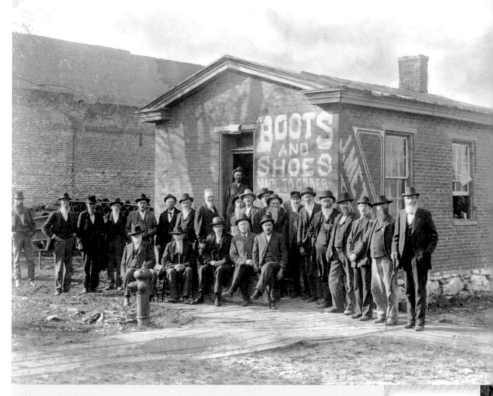

During the Civil War, raiders from the Union and the Confederate armies robbed banks in enemy-controlled towns. After the war, bushwhackers carried on robbing banks, with Jesse James becoming one of the most famous bank robbers in the late nineteenth century. Above, a group of men stand in front of a bank robbed by the James boys in Gallatin, Missouri.

One of these was in October 1866, when the bandits robbed the banking house of Alexander Mitchell & Company in Lexington, Missouri. They used a similar trick of pretending to want change for a bill, appearing to be regular customers, before pulling out their revolvers.

As the robbers fled, two other former bushwhackers, Dave and John Pool, happened to be standing outside the bank. The Pools were not part of the robbery gang. They quickly organized a posse of other former bushwhackers, and the group went in pursuit of the Clement band, but they were unsuccessful. When the posse returned, its members stated that the bandits had driven them back in a gunfight and escaped. Some people suspected the Pools of collaborating with the bandits, creating a fake posse to let the gang escape, but they denied it. One local newspaper wrote that the Pools were "swearing around the streets that they would shoot any man who dared to say they had anything to do with the robbery."

THE HUGHES & WASSON BANK

Not long after, in December 1866, Archie Clement was killed in a shootout. There is evidence that Jesse was with him when he died.

Clement had been an important person in Jesse's life, shaping the young man's future as a bandit leader. Historian T.J. Stiles writes that, with Clement's demise, Jesse James "lost his mentor, his companion in battle, and perhaps his best friend. At the same time, Clement's death opened the way for Jesse's rise to leadership, to become the man who would shake up the country."

The gang's surviving members, including Frank and Jesse, kept it going as its focus changed. A band that had been soldiers in a political and moral battle continued to transform itself into a gang of robbers intent on profit. Stiles comments, "In the months that followed Clement's death, the old Anderson guerrilla organization had increasingly descended into simple crime."

The band's numbers and membership changed as captured or killed bandits were replaced. Meanwhile, it continued to raid banks regularly for the next two years. For example, in the spring of 1867, the gang targeted a bank in Richmond, Missouri.

On a typically sleepy day in May, several small groups of strangers rode into town. No one was very concerned until about a dozen of the strangers gathered in front of the Hughes & Wasson Bank. Four of them went inside while the others stood watch. At this point, some townspeople grew suspicious. They approached the bank, and a gun battle erupted in which the mayor and two other citizens were killed. All of the bandits escaped with the money—about $3,500.

They fled into the rugged Crooked River country outside of town. A posse of 15 nearly caught up with them, and there was a running gun battle as the bandits turned and fired as they galloped, but the robbers were too swift for the posse. After outrunning the group chasing them, the band split up the money and scattered, traveling in different directions to confuse anyone who tried to pursue them.

RUSSELLVILLE

Many other robberies followed. One target was the Nimrod L. Long & Co. Bank in Russellville, Kentucky. This robbery took place in March 1868. Besides the James brothers, there were at least five others in the gang for this heist: Oliver "Ol" Shepherd, Ol's cousin George Shepherd, Arthur McCoy, John Jarrette, and Cole Younger.

Before the robbery, the men gathered at a hotel in Chaplin, Kentucky, to make their final plans. They spent a week in Russellville, quietly buying all the fast horses and guns in town, thus preventing any posse from using them.

Two days before the robbery, one of the bandits, identifying himself as Thomas Colborn of Louisville, entered the bank and asked the cashier, Nimrod Long, to make change for a large bill. When Colborn returned two days later, another man was with him. They put a revolver to Long's head and told him to empty the vault.

Somehow, Long managed to get away out the back door. He ran into the alley behind the bank and raised an alarm. A few townspeople ran, armed to defend the bank. But two mounted bandits, each with carbines, were at the front of the bank and they returned the townspeople's fire.

One citizen was injured in the shootout. The gunfire alerted other people in town, who came quickly. Not everyone realized a holdup was in progress. According to a description of the robbery in the St. Louis *Courier-Journal*, "people ran from every quarter, some bringing buckets of water under the impression that the building was afire."

Despite the citizens' efforts, the bandits got away with an estimated $12,000. Two Louisville detectives were hired to chase them, but they were hampered by the gang's habit of splitting up after a job. Nonetheless, the detectives eventually tracked down George Shepherd, who was later sentenced to three years in the state penitentiary. They also found Ol Shepherd, who died in a gunfight at his father's house.

The lead detective in the hunt for the Russellville robbers, Delos Thurman "Yankee" Bligh, was the first professional detective to hunt the James boys. In the years after, as Jesse's fame grew and he continued to elude capture, Bligh remarked that he would die happy if he could meet the robber.

According to legend, Bligh got his wish at a railroad station in Louisville, Kentucky, although the detective did not realize it until he received a postcard:

> Dear Mr. Bligh:
>
> You have been quoted as saying on more than one occasion that if you could only meet Jesse James, you'd be content to lie down and die. Well, Mr. Bligh, you can now stretch out, lie down and die. The gentleman you met the other day in the R.R. depot at Louisville was yours, sincerely,
>
> Jesse Woodson James

THE JAMES-YOUNGER GANG

Around this time, the gang that had originally been the Clement band became a more or less permanent group. This was the famous James-Younger Gang, which included, besides Frank and Jesse, another set of brothers: Cole and Jim Younger and, later, their siblings John and Bob.

Cole
Younger

Bob
Younger
(rear)

Jesse
James

Frank
James

After the death of Archie Clement and a number of senior bushwhackers, the former Clement crew became the James-Younger Gang. Membership in this new gang changed from time to time as some would briefly land in jail and the raids were carried out sporadically.

A Little Fun

Jesse James composed many letters during his career. The ones for publication used formal language, suggesting that they were rewritten or edited by others. For example, after a bank robbery in Gallatin, Missouri, in December 1869, an open letter to the state's governor from the robber was published asserting his innocence:

Some of the best men in Missouri [will vouch for me], but I well know if I was to submit to an arrest, that I would be mobbed and hanged without a trial. . . . It is true that during the war I was a Confederate soldier, and fought under the black flag [a bushwhacker symbol], but since then I have lived a peaceable citizen.

But his letters to friends showed a more relaxed side to James, such as this one sent from Texas to Jack Bishop, a former comrade in Quantrill's Raiders:

Rest Ranch, Texas
January 23, 1877

Dear Jack,
We had a little fun on the other side of the line [border] lately. A lot of [Mexicans] came over and broke up several ranches. Some of us were down that way, and "the cowboys" wanted us to help them and we done it. Some of our cattle had been taken, and I don't owe the yellow dogs anything good anyhow. Well, we left some half dozen or more for carrion-bird [vulture] meat. We brought the cattle back. I was confounded glad when we met some cavalry out after raiders. There was a big lot of them motley scamps, and we would have had a pretty rough time, I expect. But the sneaks got back as fast as they could. You would have enjoyed the racket.
As ever yours,
JWJ

The gang's membership changed over time. New outlaws were added as others moved on or were captured or killed. Meanwhile, although the gang was co-led by the Jameses and Cole Younger, one person was emerging as the dominant member. Writer Homer Croy comments, "Jesse was becoming more and more the leader. He was the most daring, he would take chances others wouldn't."

Supporting Jesse James's growing power was his love of publicity. Jesse had a penchant for writing letters to newspapers, and these put him squarely in the spotlight. He also grew increasingly confident in his abilities. Stiles comments, "He had nothing but defiance for the outside world, as he rode about, well dressed and reckless, astride an exceptional bay mare named Kate." The brash young robber was on his way to becoming famous.

FINDING FAME

Jesse James's whereabouts after the Russellville job are not known for certain. Some historians believe that he took a journey, first heading to New York City and then booking passage on the long sea route to California, where he visited an uncle. According to this story, Frank joined him, and they stopped at mining camps in Nevada before returning to Missouri.

Although the trip to California is unproven, it is true that the James boys remained out of the public eye until December 1869, when they robbed the Daviess County Savings Association in Gallatin, Missouri. The pair apparently did this job by themselves.

GALLATIN

Jesse later claimed that he and his brother targeted the Gallatin bank in the belief that its cashier was Samuel P. Cox, the Union officer who had killed Bloody Bill Anderson. The outlaw, however, may have invented this reason to make it seem as though the robbery was politically motivated. In fact, the cashier was named John W. Sheets and had no connection to Anderson.

The robbery began with the Jameses' standard ploy. Jesse entered the bank and asked for change for a $100 bill. Sheets was counting the change when Jesse pulled a revolver and shot him in the heart and head. He then held the gun on the only witness, a

After the Russellville robbery, Jesse disappeared from the public eye. Accounts say he took several trips before returning to his home in Missouri (*above*).

lawyer who happened to be in the bank. Frank entered the bank, and the brothers scooped up what they could.

The lawyer tried to escape and was shot in the arm. Nonetheless, he was able to rally others and, as the Jameses tried to flee on horseback, a dozen townspeople shot at them. When Jesse mounted his horse, it shied at the sound of a rifle and threw him off. One foot got stuck in a stirrup, and Jesse was dragged about 30 feet (9 meters) before he freed himself. The accident permanently injured his ankle.

As the horse ran off, Frank, who was already mounted, rescued Jesse, and they escaped on one horse. About a mile from town, they encountered a man and took his mount at gunpoint. The two then used both horses to escape but were bitterly disappointed when they reached safety. Their loot turned out to be only a worthless batch of paper.

CHASING THE JAMES BOYS

There was little doubt who was responsible for the crime. The runaway horse, when found, was identified as belonging to the James family. Sheriff John S. Thomason of Liberty and two deputies were given the job of riding to the James-Samuel farm in search of the robbers.

A teenage servant named Ambrose answered their knock and ran to open the stable. Frank and Jesse then burst from the stable door on horseback, their pistols drawn, and led the lawmen on a chase.

When the deputies' horses balked at jumping a fence, only Thomason could continue. He kept firing, and then dismounted to fire his last shot. He missed—and one of the James boys shot his horse. The sheriff was forced to walk back to the James farm to commandeer another mount.

The brothers returned home some time later, then rode into Kearney and angrily stormed the streets, guns at the ready. They loudly declared that they had been wrongly accused and had nothing to do with the events in Gallatin. When Thomason returned to the farm the next day with a large group of men, the brothers were long gone.

COOL, DETERMINED, DESPERATE MEN

The brazen murder in Gallatin was committed in cold blood, not self-defense. It indicated that the James brothers were not just politically motivated bushwhackers. Instead, they were bandits intent on profit, operating on their own instead of following others. T.J. Stiles writes that the deaths of their former leaders, Clement and Anderson, "forced the James brothers to decide whether to give up the guerrilla life . . . or take command for themselves. With the murder in Gallatin, they gave their answer."

The murder and robbery outraged much of Missouri. The governor offered a $500 reward for each of the bandits, nearly twice the usual amount for armed robbers. Sheets's widow, his bank, and the town and county governments posted substantial rewards as well.

The reaction among the state's newspapers was mostly anger. The St. Joseph *Gazette* commented, "Should the miscreants [criminals] be overtaken it is not probable that a jury will be required to try them. They will be shot down in their tracks, so great is the excitement among the citizens of Daviess and the adjoining counties." The Kansas City *Times*, meanwhile, noted the difficulty of catching the brothers. It stated, "They know every foot-path and by-road. . . . [T]hey are cool, determined, desperate men, well mounted and well armed."

According to some reports, the James brothers thought it wise to leave Missouri after Sheets's death. If true, it is likely that they headed to Texas or Mexico. It would have been easy for the fugitives to disappear into this open and sparsely populated region.

Legend says that they spent some time in Matamoros, a city in Mexico across the Rio Grande River from Texas. It is said that Jesse killed a Mexican man there who had gotten into a fistfight with Frank. The brothers had to shoot their way out of the brawl that followed. Four more Mexicans were killed in that fight, although the brothers were only slightly wounded. The story continues that they swam to the other side of the Rio Grande on their horses and escaped into Texas.

Whether or not they went to Mexico, the brothers did lie low for more than a year. They apparently spent some of this time in Adairsville, Kentucky, at the home of an uncle, Major George B. Hite.

Jesse was still weak from the chest wound he had received earlier, and, according to some reports, became despondent over his poor health. The bandit may even have tried to commit suicide with an overdose of morphine, a narcotic drug that is typically used as a painkiller. Given Jesse's pride and stubborn nature, however, many historians discount this story.

SHAKING STOLEN MONEY AT THE CROWD

There was no definite public sighting of the James boys until the summer of 1871. That June, they assembled a gang that probably consisted of themselves plus Cole and Jim Younger, Clell Miller, Jim White, and one other man. This group was put together to rob the Ocobock Brothers' Bank in Corydon, Iowa.

On the day of the crime, a well-known orator and clergyman, Henry Clay Dean, was in Corydon to give a speech. Almost the entire town assembled in the yard of the Methodist church to hear Dean's views on a proposed railroad line that would pass through the town.

Taking advantage of Dean's appearance, the robbers approached the bank through the nearly empty streets. Three went inside while the others stood guard. The only person in the bank, the cashier, handed over the keys to the safe at gunpoint. The robbers tied him up and left with a reported $6,000.

The gang passed the crowd in the churchyard on its way out of town. Jesse brazenly rode up and interrupted Dean's speech to announce what the gang had just done. He even dared the people of Corydon to follow them. One newspaper report asserted, "They shook the stolen money at the crowd, defying pursuit."

Most of the crowd thought the announcement was a hoax. Not until they found the cashier did the townspeople understand what had happened. A posse was quickly formed and at one point came close enough to the gang to fire shots, but the robbers eluded capture. The outlaws knew the territory well and could find shelter with some of their many nearby friends and sympathizers.

The Kansas City *Times* later published a letter from Jesse, denying that he and Frank had been involved in the robbery. He stated that they could not come forward because they feared that mobs would attack them. Meanwhile, Clell Miller was captured and arrested, but he was acquitted when witnesses swore he had been elsewhere. Eventually the search was called off.

After the Corydon robbery, the bandits followed their usual practice of splitting up and going their separate ways. According to legend, Jesse disguised himself as a farmer so well that he fooled the posse when he encountered it. He pretended to be chasing a horse thief and even rode awhile with the posse.

True or not, this story illustrates the very real difficulty authorities had in identifying the outlaws. For one thing, there were no definitive photos of the James brothers that could be used on wanted posters. Furthermore, fearing retaliation, no one around Kearney was brave enough to identify them. William A. Settle Jr. comments, "[T]he very few persons who could describe Frank and Jesse James with enough accuracy to make them identifiable on sight refused to talk. . . . Friends shielded the ex-guerrillas willingly, and others protected them out of fear."

THE COLUMBIA ROBBERY

The band struck again in April 1872. Their target this time was the Deposit Bank in the central Kentucky town of Columbia. Once again, Columbia was in a region where the James boys had plenty of relatives who could hide them.

A few days before the robbery, five strangers with good horses and fine saddles rode into nearby Adairsville and found lodging at a private home. They said they were livestock buyers, but they seemed to concentrate more on familiarizing themselves with the terrain than on inspecting any animals. These "buyers," of course, were in fact robbers: Jesse and Frank James, Cole and Jim Younger, and one more unidentified man.

On the day of the holdup, three of them, including Jesse, entered the bank while the other two stood watch. They drew their revolvers, and one bandit immediately shot the cashier point-blank—so close

Today banks have implemented all types of security measures to prevent bank robberies, including motion detectors, silent alarms, and exploding dye packs. In Jesse James' day, there was much less security other than guards and safes. Pictured is a safe that was once robbed by Jesse James.

that the gunpowder singed his shirt. Somehow, this shot was not fatal. Meanwhile, a bank customer took a swing at the bandits with a chair and was shot in the hand for his trouble. Another customer reached for a gun and was shot in the head. Two more jumped out a window, and another escaped through the door.

The wounded cashier acted bravely, refusing to open the safe. The frustrated bandits then broke open a small iron box and found cash—estimates vary from $600 to $4,000. As the bandits standing guard fired into the air to warn townspeople away, the others left the bank and then all five galloped off. Although a huge posse was formed and a reward of $2,500 was offered, once again they escaped.

THE GANG TARGETS THE FAIR

The band was growing bolder with each robbery. That fall, in September 1872, they targeted a fair, the Industrial Exposition in Kansas City, Missouri, the biggest annual fair in the state. Tens of thousands of people came yearly to the busy event. One newspaper reported, "Between the crowded sidewalks rushed hither and yon saddle horses, carriages, omnibuses, buggies, sulkies, phaetons, drags, and every imaginable variety of vehicle, drawn by every imaginable variety of horseflesh."

Frank, Jesse, and Cole brazenly rode into this packed event, wearing masks of checkered cloth that left only their eyes visible. They approached the ticket window, brandished weapons, and made off with $1,000 to $10,000 in cash (depending on the source).

During the fracas, one of the bandits fired, accidentally wounding a little girl in the leg. According to legend, Jesse later sent the girl's family a letter offering to pay her doctor bills. Some historians, however, doubt the truth of this and other details about the robbery. Historian James D. Horan comments:

> No band of outlaws "swooped down," as one newspaper declared, and from the saddle carried off a tin box containing ten thousand dollars. The cost of admission to that fair was probably less than a dollar and there must have been a large amount of small change. How then could a rider on a horse "swoop down" and pluck a box heavily weighted with ten thousand dollars in bills and coins, out of the teller's hands?

No matter what the take was, the fair job had been a remarkably daring crime, especially since a special police force was guarding the grounds. It made the front page in a number of newspapers. One admiring writer commented:

> It was one of those exhibitions of superb daring that chills the blood and transfixes the muscles of the looker-

on with a mingling of amazement, admiration, and hor-
ror.... It was a deed so high-handed, so diabolically daring and so utterly in contempt of fear that we are bound
to admire it and revere its perpetrators for the very enor-
mity of their outlawry.

The man who wrote this gushing prose was a longtime fan
of the James boys. John Newman Edwards, a former Confederate soldier, edited the *Kansas City* (Missouri) *Times*. Edwards had
met the James brothers in the spring of 1870. About the meeting,
Stiles writes, "It was the beginning of a lasting friendship that would
change the lives of all three men."

The newspaperman immediately became a loyal supporter.
He used his paper to make the gang, especially Jesse, into a potent
symbol of Confederate defiance and Southern bravery. Before the
meeting, Jesse had been unknown outside of Missouri. Without
Edwards, it is likely that he would have faded into obscurity. More
than any individual except the bandit himself, the editor made Jesse
James famous.

FACT AND FICTION

Edwards's paper was not the only one that wrote about the James
boy. Dozens of others published fanciful articles celebrating James's
supposed generosity. For example, Edwards falsely reported that the
outlaw refused to take money from ex-Confederate soldiers. James
also supposedly checked the hands of victims for calluses. Only
those with soft or manicured hands were robbed, because Jesse
would not steal from workingmen. In a typical comment about the
gang, Edwards wrote:

With them, booty is but the second thought; the wild
drama of the adventure first. These men never go upon
the highway in lonesome places to plunder the pilgrim.
That they leave to the ignoble pack of jackals.

An Admiring Newspaperman Makes Jesse James Famous

Missouri newspaper editor John Newman Edwards, a great defender of Southern guerrillas, did much to make Jesse James famous. He wrote many articles about the outlaw's supposed virtues, including one from which this is excerpted:

Jesse James . . . has a face as smooth and innocent as the face of a school girl. The blue eyes, very clear and penetrating, are never at rest. His form is tall, graceful and capable of great endurance and great effort. There is always a smile on his lips, and a graceful word or a compliment for all with whom he comes in contact. Looking at his small white hands, with their long, tapering fingers, one would not imagine that with a revolver they were among the quickest and deadliest hands in all the west. . . .

Jesse knows there is a price upon his head and . . . will [never] be taken alive. Killed—that may be. Having long ago shaken life, when death does come, [his friends] will greet him with the exclamation: "How now, old fellow."

Edwards's "facts" about the gang, repeated unquestioningly by other writers, became established parts of the James boys' legend. Not every newspaper, though, defended and glorified them. For example, the Kansas City *Daily Journal of Commerce* commented, "More audacious villains . . . or those more deserving of hanging from a limb, do not exist at this moment."

Despite such criticism, the majority of commentary—at least in Missouri—remained sympathetic to Jesse. This was true of ordinary people as well as newspapers. Robert Barr Smith comments, "If Edwards was the longest-winded and most vociferous partisan of the outlaws, he was certainly not alone. Many Missouri people felt as Edwards did, choosing to view the outlaw careers of the James-es and Youngers as a continuation of the war."

Edwards, however, had help; Jesse took a major role in his own promotion. Stiles writes, "Edwards did not simply pick out one bandit to glorify—Jesse thrust himself forward." As his fame grew, the bandit even began to tailor his robberies for maximum publicity value. Frequently, he also left behind letters to the press. Edwards or Frank James probably edited or rewrote many of these, because their style and historical references are unlikely for someone who completed only the fifth grade. In one letter, for instance, the outlaw bragged, "We are not thieves, we are bold robbers. . . . I am proud of the name, for Alexander the Great was a bold robber, and Julius Caesar, and Napoleon Bonaparte."

A DINNER INVITATION

Following the fair robbery and throughout the winter of 1872–1873, the "bold robbers" laid relatively low. Frank James and Jim Younger allegedly went to California to check out reports of gold shipments coming out of San Francisco by rail. Meanwhile, Jesse and the others robbed only one bank during this period. The heist occurred in Ste. Genevieve, Missouri. When the robbers ordered the cashier to open the safe, the only customer in the bank fled. The gang fired at him but missed.

The outlaws got away this time with an estimated $4,000 in silver. In keeping with Jesse's increasing boldness, the posse that followed the gang found a number of taunting messages along the way. One read, "Married men turn around and go home. Single men follow. We'll be in Hermann on May 30—come and have dinner with us."

True to their word, the outlaws were in the town of Hermann on the appointed night. They had dinner there and made no effort to hide their identities. No lawmen, though, came to dine with them.

By the time summer rolled around, Jesse and his comrades had a new plan. They wanted to expand their operations beyond just robbing banks. They were also going to rob trains.

5

TRAIN ROBBERS

Robbing trains had obvious advantages for bandits. The practice was smart and practical. For instance, outlaws could force locomotives to stop in remote locations far from interfering lawmen.

Train robbery was also lucrative. At that time, banks relied more heavily on cash transactions than they do today, and most regional branches sent money to their headquarters as it came to them. Railroads were the main way to transport large quantities of money and gold. Historian T.J. Stiles comments, "With clearinghouses restricted to a few large cities, a primary way to make payments and adjust balances between banks was to ship bundles of currency across the landscape."

Trains were robbed for more than just easy money; there was also the thrill. In the early 1870s, a train heist was dramatic and new. Railroads were powerful symbols of America's rapidly changing society and its reliance on technology, and they were having an enormous effect on prosperity and industrial growth. Stopping a train and taking its valuable contents could be seen as way to control and protest these societal changes.

In the South, cash transports and banks were particularly rich targets. Northern interests dominated the railroad and banking industries. Furthermore, firms called express companies, such as Wells, Fargo & Co., handled the transport of the money. Express companies were among the earliest of America's national

Trains carrying large amounts of gold and money were easy prey for outlaws in the Old West. Bandits were able to stop locomotives in remote locations by derailing them and then force the expressmen and conductors to give up their cargo. If the robbers were unsatisfied with the goods, passengers' money, jewelry, and other valuables would be added to the loot.

businesses, and to many Southerners they were simply further examples of Northern oppression.

JESSE'S FIRST TRAIN ROBBERY

The James-Younger Gang was not the first to rob a train. That distinction goes to four brothers from Indiana: John, Frank, Simon, and William Reno. The Reno brothers pulled off three daring train robberies in 1866, 1867, and 1868.

The James-Younger Gang, however, became by far the most famous train robbers. Their first exploit in this field took place in July 1873. The original plan targeted a railroad in Missouri until Frank James and Jim Younger learned that a large shipment of gold would soon be heading through Iowa, and the gang agreed to focus on it.

They chose to attack the train at an isolated spot near Adair, Iowa. The track curved sharply at this point, which would force the engineer to slow the locomotive to about 20 miles (32 km) per hour. Furthermore, the location was near a river, in a shallow depression. The banks above made an excellent hiding spot.

Wrecking the Train

The six bandits who took part in the robbery prepared for it by finding a way to stop the train. They used a crowbar and a hammer to pry a pair of the railroad track's spikes out of the ground. Then they ran ropes through holes in the rails and, holding the ropes, hid about 50 feet (15 meters) away.

The steam engine arrived on schedule. It pulled a load that included a coal car, two baggage cars, four passenger cars, and two Pullman sleeping cars. The robbers expected the shipment of gold to be in the second baggage car, guarded by an express company employee called a messenger.

As the train drew close, the bandits pulled hard on the ropes, bending the rails out of place. The engineer, John Rafferty, spotted this as the locomotive approached, and he desperately tried to stop the train. The train slowly ground to a halt, and the bandits opened fire on the engine car.

Although Rafferty saved the train's passengers from serious injury by slowing, he himself was not able to escape. The train engine toppled over as it hit the damaged rails, and the steam escaping from it scalded the engineer to death. Dennis Foley, the young fireman in charge of stoking the engine with coal, was also severely injured. He ran from the engine with his clothes on fire, rolled in the grass, and was badly burned—but not fatally.

Robbing the Train

The toppling of the locomotive had a catastrophic effect on the rest of the train. As the coal car behind the engine upended, its load spilled out. The first baggage car then jackknifed, crashing onto its side. One passenger car also came completely off the rails.

After the crash, the gang rushed to the train. They were disguised with hoods that resembled the terrifying masks worn by the Ku Klux Klan, a secret organization of proslavery terrorists. Two bandits stood guard outside, shooting whenever a face appeared in a window. Two more boarded and kept watch on the passengers. They also demanded that the terrified travelers hand over their money and valuables. The remaining two gang members, apparently including Jesse, boarded the second baggage car. One of them aimed a revolver at messenger John Burgess, who handed over the key to the safe.

The band made off with an estimated $3,000. This was a good haul, but was much less than expected. The gold shipment the robbers had hoped for had either passed through the night before or was still to come (accounts vary). The robbers also found a large shipment of precious metals, but they had no way to carry it with them.

Meanwhile, back in the passenger cars, the travelers were frightened by the wreck but mostly unhurt. Dazed or injured passengers moaned, while some screamed in fear that they would be killed by the gunmen who stood watch over them. The bandits, however, merely relieved the travelers of their money, jewelry, and other valuables.

Only about 10 minutes elapsed between the wreck and the completion of the bandits' mission. When it was over, the bandits fled and rode back to Missouri, stopping occasionally at farmhouses for meals. Robert Barr Smith comments, "They were said to have conducted themselves as gentlemen, paying for everything they got—which is not hard when you pay your bills with somebody else's money."

A $5,000 reward was posted, and a number of private detectives and posses searched extensively for the gang. As usual with this band of robbers, their pursuers were unsuccessful.

$5,000 ^{00}

REWARD

Wanted by the State of Missouri

JESSE & FRANK JAMES

For Train Robbery

Notify AUTHORITIES
LIBERTY, MISSOURI

Jesse and his gang eluded capture with help from friends, family, and former Confederates in Missouri. As a result, the authorities offered bounties or rewards for their apprehension or for information leading to their capture.

The robbery was not a complete success—the gang had missed the big gold shipment. Nonetheless, the event had historical significance. It was the first train robbery west of the Mississippi. It was also the first time an entire train, including the passengers, had been robbed. And, of course, it was the first robbery of its kind by the notorious James gang. The event caused a sensation across the United States. Stiles comments that the bold crime "reflected the Missouri raiders' rising ambitions, which were quickly rewarded with headlines nationwide."

THE GAD'S HILL ROBBERY

The whereabouts of Jesse James in the months after the Adair robbery are unknown. There is some evidence that he made an extended trip to Montana Territory. His next known exploit came in January 1874, when his gang pulled off a second train robbery in the tiny town of Gad's Hill, Missouri.

As before, the plan was carefully worked out. On the morning of the robbery, seven bandits visited a merchant in Gad's Hill and confiscated a rifle and several hundred dollars. They took the merchant at gunpoint to the Gad's Hill station, along with a handful of other townspeople.

The train station was so small that it had no building, just a platform. The robbers forced the captives, including the railroad agent, around an open fire in the chilly morning, guarding them to prevent escape. Then they used a red flag to wave down an express train headed to Little Rock, Arkansas.

As the train slowed, the bandits threw a switch that sidetracked and trapped it. The conductor jumped off, and a man in a white hood stuck a pistol in his face. The robbers placed the engineer with the other captives, and two of them forced the messenger to open his safe. They believed it held a large shipment of cash, but there was only a little more than $1,000.

"THE MOST DARING TRAIN ROBBERY ON RECORD!"

Meanwhile, the rest of the gang collected hundreds of dollars in cash and expensive items from the passengers. According to legend, one returned money taken from a minister and asked the clergy-man to pray for them; they also supposedly let the conductor keep his watch because the man claimed it was a treasured present.

The outlaws departed on horseback after telling the engineer that he could continue on his journey. When the train reached Pied-mont, Missouri, news of the robbery was immediately sent out by telegraph.

With his love of publicity, James left an already prepared notice for the press at the station. This announcement was accurate in its description of the robbery, clear evidence that it had been carefully planned. The robber even provided a blank space for the amount stolen and courteously deleted an expletive:

THE MOST DARING TRAIN ROBBERY ON RECORD!

The southbound train of the Iron Mountain Railroad was stopped here this evening by five heavily armed men and robbed of _____ dollars. The robbers arrived at the station a few minutes before the arrival of the train and arrested the agent and put him under guard and then threw the train on the switch. The robbers were all large men, all being slightly under six feet. After robbing the train they started in a southerly direction. They were all mounted on handsome horses. There is a h--- of an excitement in this part of the country.

"SHELL OUT"

The James-Younger Gang did not always limit itself to trains and banks. The robbers sometimes also held up stagecoaches, which travelers in the West often used to reach areas not served by railroads.

One of these holdups occurred near Hot Springs, Arkansas, in January 1874, the same month as the Gad's Hill heist. The men

An Exciting Adventure

Adventure books called dime novels were popular entertainment during the period of the Old West. Many fanciful fictions were written about Jesse James's exploits, such as D.W. Stevens' *The James Boys in Minnesota*, published in 1882. Here is an excerpt from Stevens' book:

> The cold steel-like glitter which had been indelibly stamped in their eyes, on that summer day in 1861, when Jesse's back smarted under blows, and he swore to wipe out the indignity with blood, seemed to become colder and harder, as they reflected on what the night might bring forth.
>
> "Jesse, we are in a nest of robbers," said Frank.
>
> "Yes, and murderers," replied Jesse. "We must teach them a lesson."
>
> "I think so."
>
> "We must wipe the entire bloodthirsty set [Northerners] from the face of existence! It's a duty we owe society," said Jesse, with a light laugh. "We are working now wholly for the benefit of society."
>
> "Yes," replied Frank, without the least bit of humor in his voice.
>
> "It may be that by ridding the world of such wretches, Frank, that we may find a balance accounts for some of our own missteps."

who pulled this off were probably the James brothers, Cole and Jim Younger, and Clell Miller. Another stagecoach holdup, in April, involved a different group, probably the Jameses, Arthur McCoy, Jim Greenwood, and Jim Reed. This robbery involved the regular mail stage between Austin and San Antonio, Texas. A number of distinguished people were traveling on it, including a bishop and the president of the First National Bank of San Antonio.

All of the passengers were robbed, with the bank president losing about $1,000 in cash. The robbers were apparently courteous toward the women on board, although the gang members warned that the women would be searched if they did not give up their jewelry and money. Before leaving, the bandits cut loose several of the stagecoach's horses so that it would take the driver longer to reach Austin.

As usual, accounts of this and other robberies were often exaggerated—but they make good stories nonetheless. According to legend, for instance, the gang returned a gold watch and chain to a passenger on the Hot Springs coach after realizing that he was a former Confederate soldier. Another story has it that one of the bandits reminded the bishop on the Texas coach that the Bible advises people not to carry money while traveling. "Therefore," the robber said, "we propose to put you back into the good graces of the Lord. Shell out."

TRYING TO ORGANIZE A SPECIAL POSSE

The problem of capturing the James-Younger Gang was becoming increasingly serious. Many newspapers and private citizens in Missouri were sympathetic to the gang. Furthermore, many state officials turned a blind eye to the robbers. The St. Louis *Republican* wrote, "For ten years the JAMES brothers and YOUNGER brothers have robbed and murdered in this and adjacent states with absolute impunity. . . . Judges, sheriffs, constables and the whole machinery of law are either set at defiance by a gang of villains, or bought or frightened into neutrality."

Under pressure, the government of Missouri began to work harder than before to bring the gang to justice. Governor Silas Woodson told his fellow politicians, "The law is inadequate. The authorities are powerless to deal with these outlaws. Life and property are unsafe. The time has come to put an end to these conditions of affairs that have become uncontrollable."

Woodson persuaded the state legislature to approve the creation of a special organization consisting of 25 men who would be devoted solely to rounding up the bandits. Plans for this special group, however, were held up by political wrangling, and the organization was never created.

THE PINKERTON AGENTS

The express companies were more serious about catching the James-Younger Gang than the politicians. After all, it was mostly their money that was being stolen. In the wake of the Gad's Hill robbery, one of these firms, the Adams Express Company, turned to the National Detective Agency for help.

This agency, founded by Allan Pinkerton in Chicago, was the largest and most famous agency of its kind in the nation. "The Pinks," as its agents were known, were smart, tough, and relentless. They had brought satisfaction to their clients in scores of cases.

In this instance, however, they were unsuccessful. One of the first "Pinks" sent to find the Jameses met with a quick death. This was John Whicher, who was still in his twenties. Whicher arrived in Liberty, Missouri, near the James-Samuel farm, in March 1874.

The detective was confident that he could capture the bandits single-handedly. A local bank president and a former sheriff both tried to stop him from directly confronting the Jameses. The former sheriff reportedly said, "The old woman would kill you if the boys don't." Despite this warning, Whicher remained confident. He left Liberty, bound for the James-Samuel farm, dressed as a farmhand looking for work.

The next morning, a traveler found the agent's body on the road about a half-mile from the farm. He had bullet wounds in his head and heart. Rewards for the killer or killers were posted but never claimed. It was widely assumed that someone in the James brothers' extensive network of friends and family had tipped the boys off about the approaching Pinkerton agent.

As soon as news of the killing reached his office in Chicago, Allan Pinkerton sent another agent to retrieve Whicher's body. He also dispatched two more agents to seek out the Youngers in St. Clair County, with a local sheriff as a guide.

This trio happened to stop at a farmhouse where two of Cole's younger brothers were staying. The three lawmen, all heavily armed, aroused the Youngers' suspicions, and the bandits followed them as they departed. When the brothers ordered the three strangers to stop, the men took off at a gallop.

Both of the Pinkerton agents and the sheriff were killed in the ensuing battle. John Younger, shot through the neck, also died. His brother Jim was the only survivor. Jim alerted a neighbor about the gunfight and asked him to take care of John's body as he left.

"TAKEN AT LAST"

Later that year, an important date in Jesse James's personal life arrived. He and his cousin Zee, who had nursed him during his recuperation from his chest wound, had long been attracted to each other. For nine years, they carried on a prolonged courtship. Finally, in April 1874, Jesse and petite, dark-haired, quiet Zee were married. She was 29; Jesse would soon turn 27.

The ceremony was held at the home of Zee's older sister, Lucy Browder, in Kearney. Zee's family did not approve of her marriage to a notorious outlaw, even if he was family. A minister who was an uncle to both of them officiated, but only after Jesse had convinced him of his innocence of criminal activity. (It does not appear that Jesse kept his profession a secret from Zee.) A few months later, in June, Frank James also married. His bride was a schoolteacher, Anne Ralston.

Jesse's supporter in the press, John Newman Edwards, published a story about the outlaw's marriage in the St. Louis *Dispatch*, where the editor now worked. As always, Edwards was

Jesse and Zee had two children who survived to adulthood, Jesse Jr. and Mary Susan (*above*). Jesse Jr. became a respected lawyer in Kansas City, Missouri.

enthusiastic in his prose. The headline ran: "CAPTURED: The Celebrated Jesse W. James Taken at Last. His Captor a Woman, Young, Accomplished, and Beautiful."

Jesse and Zee spent the first months of their married life in Texas with relatives. Their first child was born in August 1875. They named him Jesse Edwards James, the middle name probably in honor of John Edwards. The couple had three more children: twin sons, born in 1877, who died after only five days, and a daughter, Mary Susan, born in 1879.

"GOOD-BYE, BOYS"

The year 1874 ended as it had begun for the gang, with a string of robberies. One, in tiny Muncie, Kansas, used a plan that was similar to the one used in Gad's Hill.

The train station in Muncie also did duty as a general store and post office. When the bandits came to town, a few of them held virtually the entire town prisoner in this building while others piled railroad ties on the track. They flagged down the train as it passed through, pulled the fireman and engineer to the ground, and forced them to uncouple the baggage car.

The outlaws then boarded this car and forced the messenger at gunpoint to open the safe. It contained roughly $18,000 in currency and $5,000 in gold. The bandits also found more cash and jewelry inside the mailbag. The total was later estimated at $30,000.

Before leaving with this haul, the bandits stopped a man who was riding by and forced him to give up his fresh horse. Supposedly one of the robbers told the hapless train employees before fleeing, "Good-bye, boys, no hard feelings. We have taken nothing from you."

THE PINKERTONS
IN PURSUIT

The James-Younger Gang's exploits were becoming increasingly bold. Allan Pinkerton, the detective, was furious at his lack of success in finding the bandits. He took the case on personally, rather than entrusting it to his employees.

Early in 1875, Pinkerton assembled a team of operatives for a sneak attack on the James family farm. He had information that Frank and Jesse were in the house at the time, along with Clell Miller and at least one other member of the gang.

Just after midnight on the freezing cold night of January 24 (or 25 or 26—accounts vary), small groups of lawmen gathered around the farmhouse. These groups were a combination of Pinkerton agents and local lawmen. They called out for Frank and Jesse, assuring those inside that they were surrounded.

THE EXPLOSION

When there was no response from inside the home, the detectives went to work. Two of them approached the house with incendiary devices. According to some sources, these were railroad lamps filled with coal oil or kerosene and lit with wicks extending out of them. Other sources refer to an iron ball that was wrapped in cotton and filled with combustible material.

In any case, the devices were intended to start fires, illuminate a darkened area, or both. The men battered down a boarded-up window and threw their devices in. Ambrose, a teenage servant in the house, saw the men and tried to raise an alarm. He later recalled:

> I heard noise in the northwest corner of the kitchen, and men talking. I then raised up in my bed and saw a light glimmering through a crack in the panel of the door. I then got up . . . looking toward the north window, and saw two men, either one or the other or both with a light in their hands; they then raised a ball or something that was red and threw it at the window, which knocked me down. It then fell on the floor, and an oily substance ran out over the floor.

Dr. Reuben Samuel, Jesse's stepfather, tried to counteract the iron ball's danger by sweeping it with a broom into the fireplace. He thought that this might contain any damage. Unfortunately, his idea backfired—the heat of the fire caused the ball to explode.

After the explosion, there was a brief but intense gunfight before Frank and Jesse fled on horseback. One Pinkerton agent was wounded and later died en route to Chicago. Some sources say that Ambrose, the teenage servant, was the one who inflicted the wound.

Most of Jesse's family escaped the blast and gunfight, and the house was not destroyed, but there were still tragic results. The explosion slightly injured Ambrose and sent a piece of metal tearing into Zerelda Samuel's right arm. The mother of the James boys was so badly injured that her arm was later amputated at the elbow to prevent gangrene. Worst of all, the explosion killed the youngest family member, Jesse and Frank's four-year-old half-brother, Archie.

Scottish detective and spy Allan Pinkerton founded the Pinkerton National Detective Agency in 1850 and then became famous when he foiled a plot to assassinate President-elect Abraham Lincoln. In 1874, the agency was hired to stop the James-Younger Gang, which Pinkerton took on as a personal mission.

Pinkerton later denied that he had intended to burn the house or hurt anyone. He stated that the combustible material thrown was not meant to start a fire, that he simply wanted to light up the inside of the farmhouse so that his agents could see the occupants inside.

It appears, however, that Pinkerton did intend all along to cause an explosion. The evidence includes a letter that later surfaced, in which he expressed his intention to do just that. Perhaps Pinkerton only wanted to harm or capture the James brothers, but events got out of control. William A. Settle Jr. comments, "That the detectives intended to endanger the lives of a whole family is doubtful; but the deaths of [the earlier Pinkerton agents] had made them desperate, and they were careless."

AN APPARENT REVENGE KILLING

Allan Pinkerton and others in the group that attacked the farmhouse were later indicted for the murder of young Archie Samuel. No arrests were carried out, though, and the charges were eventually dropped. It appears, however, that there was at least one instance of revenge on the Pinkerton outfit after the raid.

Dan Askew was a neighbor of the James-Samuel family. He had for some time secretly sheltered the Pinkerton agents, allowing them to use his farm as a base and passing on information to the detectives. Soon after the raid, Askew was shot to death while carrying water from a spring to his house. Although the killers were never found, the James brothers were natural suspects.

Public sentiment was overwhelmingly in favor of the Jameses in the wake of the raid. Many people were outraged at what they saw as a vicious attack on an entire family—an attack that killed a young boy but failed in its primary mission of capturing Frank and Jesse.

HUNDREDS OF NEW FRIENDS

In fact, it is likely that the fiasco did a great deal to burnish Jesse James's reputation as a sympathetic figure. George Patton, the sheriff of Clay County, dryly commented at the time, "The grand move has made hundreds of friends for the James boys, when they had but few." Many modern historians agree with this assessment.

Newspapers around the country picked up the story and, once again, the James brothers became national news. Even a number of Northern newspapers were sympathetic to the bandits—or at least

Hiding from the Pinkertons

The James-Younger Gang excelled at hiding from their pursuers. Writer Homer Croy notes:

They rarely hid in the woods, unless hard-pressed. They never carried blankets or bedrolls, or anything else that might slow them up when they wanted to be quickly on their way. Anyhow, they were nearly always under shelter. Sometimes they would be registered at country hotels just like any normal cattle buyers, and pay their bills. Sometimes it would be in a church or a schoolhouse. . . . But the great protection was friends and relatives.

Meanwhile, one of the gang's hunters, Pinkerton agent L.E. Angell, recalled:

The people [near the James home] are so afraid they would not tell where they were if they knew. They would hide themselves, and when they talk about them they assume a mysterious air, talk in low whispers, and you will have to get them into a back room before they will say anything, then they don't dare tell half they know.

disapproved of Pinkerton's tactics. Typical of this was the *New York Times*, which wrote, "Everyone condemns the barbarous method used by the detectives."

John Newman Edwards, the newspaper editor who had written admiringly for years about Jesse James and his gang, wrote predictably fiery prose about the attack. He urged the people of Missouri to hunt the detectives down like animals. Edwards thundered, "Men of Missouri, you who fought under Anderson, Quantrill . . . and the balance of the borderers and guerrillas . . . give up these scoundrels [the Pinkertons] to the Henry Rifle and Colt's revolver."

SYMPATHY FOR THE OUTLAWS

Legislation put before the Missouri state government showed how strong public sentiment was running in favor of the bandits. By this time, former Confederates were again allowed to vote and to hold public office, and a number of them were in the legislature.

These pro-Southern politicians sponsored a bill that explicitly praised the James-Younger Gang. It also offered the gang members amnesty from any wartime crimes, if they agreed to stand trial for crimes committed afterward. The bill was taken very seriously, and was only narrowly defeated when the legislature voted on it.

The pro-Confederate forces in the state government did succeed on another front. They were able to push through legislation that set a low limit on any rewards that the governor offered for bandits. This protected the outlaws, because small rewards were not powerful incentives for people to betray the criminals.

A NEW IDENTITY

Not long after the Pinkerton raid, Jesse and Zee James left Missouri. It is likely that they feared their continued presence might expose Zerelda to further danger. Jesse sometimes claimed that he had been forced into the outlaw life and had no alternative but to continue, since it was the only life he had ever led. The bandit allegedly commented, "They wouldn't let me stay at home, and what else can I do?"

The Jameses first moved to Edgefield, Tennessee. They took new names, calling themselves Josie and John Davis Howard. Assuming a new identity was a relatively easy thing to do in those days. Also, few people far away from Kearney would have been able to recognize the famous outlaw, since photos of the James boys were rare. (As far as is known, no "Wanted" posters have survived into modern times.) Only descriptions and sketches, which were often inaccurate, existed to identify them.

Furthermore, no fingerprinting techniques or other sophisticated identification methods existed at the time. Also helping them was the slow and unreliable nature of communicating or traveling from one town to another. It was therefore fairly easy for the James family to change their names and roam the land with relative freedom.

MORE IDENTITIES

Jesse James identified himself to people in Tennessee as a wheat speculator, someone who bought and sold grain. This job provided a plausible reason for his frequent absences, which often lasted for weeks at a time.

Some of those absences included trips with his brother that did not involve robbery but were purely for pleasure. For example, he and Frank apparently spent time during this period in Saratoga Springs, New York, which was then a fashionable gambling town. They were also reported to have visited Long Branch, New Jersey, and New York City. According to some sources, Frank attended the theater in these cities while Jesse gambled or played the horses.

Along the way, they are reputed to have taken several aliases. At one point, for instance, Jesse was William Campbell, a Texas cattleman. It is also said that in New York City he identified himself as Charles Lawson of England. This seems unlikely, however, considering the difficulty someone like Jesse—who spent most of his life in Missouri and only got through the fifth grade—would have in believably faking a British accent.

ROCKY CUT

Late in 1875 the gang reassembled and committed another bank robbery in Huntington, West Virginia, but evidence indicates that Jesse James was not present. His wife had given birth shortly before the holdup to their first child, Jesse Jr., so this is a plausible conclusion.

The winter of 1875–1876 passed quietly for the gang. In the summer of 1876, however, Jesse James rejoined his colleagues in crime. One escapade took place in July: a train robbery on the Missouri-Pacific line. They decided to stop the train at Rocky Cut, an isolated spot where a bridge was being built near Otterville, Missouri.

The bandits commandeered a small farmhouse nearby to use as a headquarters. They then took the train watchman at the Rocky Cut depot captive and tied him up. They prepared to derail the train by piling ties on the track and loosening the rails. Six of the robbers then stood by the track while two others stayed with the horses. Some of them wore bandannas; others donned cloth masks that covered their entire heads.

FINDING THE KEY

The bandits used the watchman's lantern to wave down the train. The engineer stopped the locomotive when he saw the light and the debris that blocked his path. When the train stopped, three men climbed into the express car. The door was already open, because the baggage master and messenger wanted to enjoy the evening breeze on the hot summer night.

There were two safes in the express car. When it became clear that a robbery was under way, the messenger fled to the front of the train. He gave the key to one of the safes to the brakeman. The brakeman hid the key in his shoe, and the messenger tried to hide himself among the passengers.

The robbers discovered that the key was missing and forced the engineer and fireman into the baggage car. They lined these prisoners against the wall along with the baggage master. The bandits forced the baggage master, at gunpoint, to identify the messenger, who in turn confessed that he had given the key to the brakeman.

Once the bandits retrieved the key, they were able to open one safe. But there was no key for the second safe, so they tried to break it open with a pick taken from the engine car. They managed to

DETECTIVE LIBRARY

No. 576. COMPLETE | FRANK TOUSEY, Publisher, 34 & 36 North Moore Street, New York. | PRICE 10 CENTS | Vol. I.

The Subscription Price of DETECTIVE LIBRARY by the year is $5.00; $2.50 per six months post-paid. Address FRANK TOUSEY, Publisher, 34 & 36 North Moore Street, New York. Box 2730.

THE JAMES BOYS' COMPACT;

OR,

Carl Greene's Strange Adventures at the Deserted House.

By D. W. STEVENS.

Jesse claimed that he had no alternative but to be an outlaw once the authorities were after him. He continued his life of crime with his gang, robbing the Missouri-Pacific line in the summer of 1876, depicted on the cover of this boys' adventure magazine. Another Younger brother, Bruce, and Hobbs Kerry were arrested for the train holdup.

break a small hole in it, through which one robber reached inside and pulled out handfuls of currency.

Meanwhile, the passengers cowered in their seats as an armed bandit kept an eye on them. One passenger, a minister, prayed loudly and led the group in singing hymns to comfort and calm them. Settle comments that this group singing was "an accompaniment to robbery odd enough to unnerve most bandits."

After stealing the passengers' money and valuables, the bandits allowed the train to continue. When it reached the nearby town of Tipton, Missouri, the conductor wired his superiors in St. Louis, Sedalia, and Kansas City. Posses rushed to the area, but —as usual— the robbers were long gone. Their take was an estimated $15,000 to $17,000 from the safes, plus an unknown amount from the passengers.

THE NEXT JOB

Soon after the Rocky Cut job, the gang began to plan another robbery. For this adventure, eight men were needed. This time the core group consisted of six longtime members—the James brothers and Clell Miller, plus Bob, Jim, and Cole Younger. Accompanying them were two new recruits: Charlie Pitts and William Stiles, who also went by the alias Bill Chadwell.

The target was the First National Bank of Northfield, Minnesota. It was supposedly chosen because the gang believed that it had a connection to a prominent ex-Union general and politician. T.J. Stiles comments:

> [T]he operation . . . was the most significant of their outlaw careers. Not because of the money involved— no unusually large haul awaited them at their chosen destination—nor because of the great distance from their Missouri birthplaces—Huntington, West Virginia, had been just as far. It was because of who they were coming to rob, here in the far North, a target of truly

national significance: former general, senator, and governor Adelbert Ames.

The Northfield raid was destined to become the most daring and infamous of all the robberies the James-Younger Gang committed. It was also the adventure that spelled the end for the renowned gang.

7

THE NORTHFIELD DISASTER

Northfield was the ripe target for a band of bold robbers. According to T.J. Stiles, the town was "the perfect target for a man with a gun."

Northfield was sleepy, affluent, and populated mainly by law-abiding Scandinavian immigrants. It was already the home of several small colleges. Robert Barr Smith writes:

> It was a peaceful sort of place, the kind of orderly hamlet where nobody carried a gun. It was a busy mill town, the heart of prosperous farm country, so the outlaws expected there would be lots of money in the bank, ripe for the picking. And the town was small, so they assumed it would be easy to ride clear in a hurry after cleaning out the bank. Moreover, the town had only one bank, which meant all the money was handily collected in one place.

GETTING READY

Jesse James estimated that the gang could net $75,000 with relative ease. Not everyone in the gang agreed, however; Cole and Jim

75

Bob was the thirteenth of fourteen Younger children. When he was a young boy, Bob witnessed his father's murder by Union soldiers and his home burned to the ground. Bob later followed his brothers Cole, Jim, and John by joining the James-Younger Gang.

Younger opposed the plan, calling it too dangerous. Besides, they were planning to give up the outlaw life. They wanted to marry their sweethearts in a double wedding and settle in Texas to raise cattle.

Cole and Jim changed their minds when their younger brother Bob announced that he was determined to go along on the adventure. Worried about him, the other Youngers reluctantly agreed to the plan.

It appears that the bandits traveled to Minnesota in small groups to evade suspicion. They probably went by train to avoid exhausting the horses. This supposition is borne out by the knowledge that when they bought horses in Minnesota they apparently did not sell any others.

A few weeks before the robbery, the group met in the small town of Owatonna to finalize their plans, and then split up. They traveled to Minneapolis by different routes, again probably by train, and rendezvoused in late August. They bought horses and spent some time at a secluded farmhouse, training the animals to be unafraid of gunfire. Then the outlaws split up again and took different routes to another small town, Mankato, on September 2. The groups found lodging in various hotels and a private home. They spent a few days drinking and playing poker in town.

Apparently, the robbers had initially targeted a bank in Mankato. As they rode into town, however, they spotted a large gathering near the bank. A man in the crowd pointed to the riders and said something, which made others turn and look.

The bandits suspected a trap. They canceled their plan and moved on to Northfield. According to several sources, however, the crowd in Mankato was simply watching some construction, and the man who pointed was simply remarking on the fine horses the outlaws rode. As with so much about the James-Younger legend, the details of this story may not be true.

Scouting

The gang spent several days scouting the area around Northfield. They separated again into groups and stayed in two nearby towns, Janesville and Faribault. Some of them told local townspeople that they were interested in buying a farm. They used this story as a pretext to ask people closely about the region and its inhabitants.

Early in the morning of September 7, they met in a wooded area to finalize plans. They decided to split up and approach the town from different directions, so they could investigate escape routes more thoroughly. Also, it would have been suspicious if eight men were seen riding together.

Many details are fuzzy about what happened in the hours before the raid. Smith writes, "It is most probable that the gang rode toward the bank in three units, as they had planned."

Three men—probably Frank, Bob Younger, and Charlie Pitts—were to ride quietly into town and enter the bank. Meanwhile, Cole Younger and Clell Miller, two blocks behind them, would take up lookout positions outside the building. Jesse James, Jim Younger, and William Stiles were to stay near a bridge across the Cannon River, which bisected the town. They would wait in reserve in case there were complications.

The signal for trouble would be a single gunshot. If the robbery went smoothly, the bandits would rendezvous in the town of Rochester before splitting up and heading for Missouri. Stiles would guide them as they left the state; he had once lived in Minnesota and knew the terrain.

Their target was part of a large building called the Scriver Block. It was on one corner of Bridge Square, on the east side of the river. Behind the building was an alley that also ran behind two hardware stores. Across the street was a hotel called the Dampier House.

Setting the Stage

Around 2 P.M., the outlaws rode to their assigned positions. They wore long coats called linen dusters, which were popular among horse riders because they kept trail dust off their clothes. The dusters were especially handy for bandits, since the coats hid guns and ammunition.

Frank James, Charlie Pitts, and Bob Younger dismounted as planned in front of the bank. They walked to the corner, rested on

The robbery of the First National Bank in Northfield, Minnesota, turned out to be the turning point for the James-Younger Gang. The citizens of Northfield defended their bank and became involved in a shootout with the gang. Only Jesse and Frank would make it back to safety in Missouri. Pictured is a 1948 picture of the Jesse James Café, which was the site of the Northfield bank robbery.

some wooden boxes in front of one of the hardware stores, and began idly whittling small pieces of wood. Smith comments, "They tried to look as nonchalant as possible—at least for three strangers in long dusters."

When they saw Miller and Cole Younger approach to act as lookouts, the three entered the bank. Cole Younger dismounted in front of the bank and pretended to adjust his saddle. Miller went to the bank door and looked in, then closed the door and walked back and forth in front of it.

INSIDE THE BANK

Meanwhile, the robbers inside took their revolvers from under their long coats, jumped over the counter, and told the three startled bank employees to get on their knees. One employee, Alonzo Bunker, remarked that he thought the robbery was a joke until he saw their guns: "Looking those revolvers in the face, the hole in each of them seemed about as large as a hat."

The bandits demanded that the vault be opened so they could get at the safe. The acting cashier, Joseph Heywood, replied that the vault was open but the safe was on a time lock and he could not open it. In fact, the safe was not on a time lock. Furthermore, its combination lock had not been twirled. The robbers could have opened it just by turning the handle.

When one of the bandits entered the vault, Heywood managed to slam the door shut. Another bandit seized the cashier by the collar and forced him to let the trapped bandit out. Heywood then tried to shout an alarm, but a gunman hit him on the head with the butt of a revolver. Increasingly angered by Heywood's refusal to open the safe, the robbers also made a superficial cut on his throat and fired a gun close to his head in an attempt to scare him into submission.

While the bandits were trying to force Heywood to open the safe, Bunker was able to escape, crashing through the back door into the alley. One of the bandits followed and shot Bunker in the shoulder. The bullet, though, missed his vital organs, and he was able to escape.

The frustrated bandits rifled through all the papers they could find but saw nothing of value. In their haste, they missed two counter drawers full of money—about $15,000.

As they were frantically searching, the robbers heard gunfire outside and realized they had to get out right away. As they fled, one of them climbed onto a desk and shot Heywood point-blank in the head. Frank James may have been the killer, but this has never been proven.

THE TOWN SQUARE BECOMES A BATTLEGROUND

Meanwhile, the residents of the town had become suspicious of the men standing outside the bank. When a local merchant approached the front door, the bandits handled him roughly and told him to get away. The lookouts then fired their guns in the air to summon the last three bandits.

They came riding into town, firing their own guns. Their purpose was to distract and scare the townspeople. However, many citizens were not yet aware of the robbery, so they were not alarmed by the gunfire. Smith comments, "Some took the strangers to be hunters in town for the prairie chicken season, then in full swing. Others believed the riders had something to do with the promotion of a circus or Wild West show."

As the townspeople realized what was happening, however, the situation became chaotic. Northfield's church bells began to ring an alarm, and several citizens armed themselves and converged on the bank. Soon, James D. Horan writes, "The square . . . had been turned into a battleground."

Up at Carleton College, a small private school, the order was given to "keep the girls off the street." (Carleton's students were both men and women.) A professor's wife took the female students to an upper floor. One student commented, "Every girl was to take an axe and we went all of us to the third floor, determined to make a good resistance."

Back at the square, a young medical student, Henry M. Wheeler, was home from the University of Michigan for a visit. He was sitting in a chair in front of his father's drugstore when the robbery occurred. Wheeler ran to the bank, but Clell Miller pointed a revolver at him and ordered the young man to keep away.

Wheeler ran back to his father's store to find a gun, then changed his mind and ran to the Dampier House. He found an old shotgun and four cartridges there and climbed to the fourth floor. The medical student was able to fatally shoot Miller as the outlaw tried to mount his horse.

THE STREETS WERE QUIET NOW

In the gun battle, Stiles was also shot dead as was Pitts's horse. Cole Younger, already mounted, was shot in the thigh, and Bob Younger was hit in the elbow. Nonetheless, Cole was able to rescue his brother, and Bob swung onto Cole's horse behind him. The surviving bandits made their getaway. The gun battle was over as quickly as it had begun. Smith writes:

> The streets of Northfield were quiet now, save for the barking of dozens of dogs and the frenzied clanging of every bell in town, and the citizens began to leave cover to wander down Division Street and stare at the detritus [debris] of war. A horse lay dead near the bank, and two strange men in bloody linen dusters lay sprawled in the street. . . . The façades of the downtown buildings were pocked with ragged scars of bullet strikes; broken window glass littered the street.

The townspeople found another casualty besides the bank cashier. Nicolaus Gustafson (or Gustavson), a Swedish immigrant, had come to town to shop for supplies. Gustafson, who spoke little English, apparently did not understand when people shouted at him to take cover. He was shot in the head and lingered for several days before dying.

The dead robbers were unfamiliar to the townspeople, so their bodies were not immediately identified. They were kept overnight in a vacant building and brought into the street the next day so people could see them. Meanwhile, the town kept up an armed vigil for several days in case the robbers returned.

The gang members had left so quickly that they had not cut the town's telegraph wires as planned. News of the robbery spread, and bank officials and the state government announced handsome rewards for the capture of the outlaws. Hundreds of men formed posses, and the most widespread manhunt in Minnesota's history sprang into action. Unfortunately, the reward money lured many amateurs, whose ineptness and disorganization hindered the professionals on the case.

A TOUGH ESCAPE

The six survivors—the Youngers, the James brothers, and Pitts— were at a serious disadvantage. Those who were injured kept the gang from moving quickly, and they were also forced to abandon their exhausted horses. As they made their way, the bandits could sometimes steal horses, but often they were on foot.

Unable to risk shelter, they had to stay mainly in the open, and the autumn weather turned bad on them. The outlaws had to slog for days through seemingly endless rain and mud. Furthermore, they were in unknown territory and no longer had Stiles to act as their guide.

According to legend, Jesse wanted to leave Bob and Jim Younger behind. He thought that the telltale trails of blood they left were a danger to the others. There is no proof of this, but Jesse and Cole did get into an argument over something. It nearly resulted in a shootout, but ended when the James boys went a separate way.

The Youngers' bad luck continued. They were recognized when they stopped at a farmhouse for food. The farmer's teenage son rode

8 miles (13 kilometers) to the nearest town, Madelia, and notified the authorities.

CAPTURED!

A posse led by James Glispin, the county sheriff, confronted them. There was a gunfight and Pitts was killed. The Youngers were badly injured—reportedly, Cole suffered 11 bullet wounds.

The surviving bandits were taken to Madelia. People came from all around to see the famous prisoners. Their capture was a sensation—probably the biggest thing that had ever happened in Madelia.

After recovering from their wounds, the Youngers were put in jail in nearby Faribault to await trial. Newsmen, detectives, and scores of curious citizens converged there. Authorities had to step in at one point to prevent a mob from attacking the captives.

The bandits were charged with the murder of Gustafson, the Swedish immigrant, and complicity in the murder of Heywood, the cashier. By pleading guilty they avoided the death penalty. They were sentenced instead to life imprisonment at the state prison in Stillwater.

This left the James boys as the only bandits still on the run. They were slowly heading south through Iowa toward Missouri, surviving by sleeping in the open and eating stolen crops and chickens. Despite their hardships, the brothers avoided capture and reached safety. Stiles comments, "They had outrun, outfought, and outsmarted perhaps a thousand pursuers, crossing hundreds of miles of hostile territory. And they had survived."

WHAT WENT WRONG

By any reckoning, the Northfield raid was a disastrous failure for the gang. Everyone but the James boys was dead or captured, and the take from the bank had been a paltry $26 or so.

One great question remained unanswered: How did a well-organized and experienced band of professional robbers fail so badly? In a statement made after his capture, Cole Younger blamed the catastrophe on the too-high spirits of some of the gang.

The men in the bank had apparently shared a quart of whiskey beforehand. This may have been a story Cole concocted or exaggerated to explain why the raid had failed. However, F.J. Wilcox, one of the bank employees, remembered a distinct smell of whiskey coming from the robbers.

Another factor in the gang's failure was that they were in unknown territory and far from home, away from the network of friends and relatives who could have hidden them. Furthermore, they had woefully little firepower. They had carried none of their usual rifles, only handguns. This suggests that the gang was dangerously overconfident. Stiles comments, "[T]he Northfield robbery would be forever remembered . . . as the day Jesse James reached beyond his grasp."

MEXICO

Once out of Minnesota, the James brothers wanted to avoid going straight home to Missouri. According to various sources, they went to Kentucky and holed up with friends and relatives. They also spent some time in a rugged part of west Texas and crossed the Rio Grande River into Mexico.

There are many stories about the James brothers' adventures in Mexico, some of them possibly even true. According to legend, at one point they visited a wide-open border town called Piedras Negras. There they were attacked by a mob seeking revenge for the death of a man the brothers had killed earlier. Frank and Jesse managed to fight them off in a furious gun battle, killing four men. Jesse supposedly suffered a minor bullet wound during this fight—his first injury since the Civil War.

Another story involved a friend from their days as bushwhackers. This man had married a Mexican woman in the town of Monclova, and the couple sponsored a dance in honor of the James boys. The bandits tried to hide their identities, but two men recognized them and alerted a nearby Mexican military brigade.

The soldiers surrounded the house where the dance was in progress and demanded the bandits' surrender. But Frank and Jesse were better shots than the military men. In the gunfight that followed, they escaped back to Texas.

When the famous outlaws finally returned home, they essentially had to start all over again. Their gang of trusted comrades was gone. It was time for the next and last chapter in Jesse James's life to begin.

THE ASSASSINATION OF JESSE JAMES BY THE COWARD ROBERT FORD

When the James boys returned to the States, they moved to Nashville, Tennessee. There, they adopted new identities to hide from the law. Jesse was "Thomas Howard" and Frank was "B.J. Woodson."

TRYING A NEW LIFE

For some time, Frank had hoped to abandon the outlaw life. He wanted to settle down with his wife and their son, Robert Franklin. Frank bought a farm and joined a Methodist church.

Like his brother, Jesse briefly tried his hand at a normal life. It was easy to be "Mr. Howard"—no one in Tennessee, except for his family, knew what he looked like beyond a general description. As a result, he remained anonymous for some time. According to James D. Horan, "In Nashville, Jesse's disguise was so complete that on one occasion he entered his horse at a state fair and rode it himself to win a prize. No one recognized him, though detectives thronged the fair grounds."

But abiding by the law bored him, and in 1879 he formed a new gang. Among its members were Jesse's cousin Wood Hite and Clell Miller's younger brother, Ed, along with Bill Ryan, Tucker Bassham, and Dick Liddil.

One crime the new gang pulled off, in October 1879, was the robbery of a train near Glendale, Missouri. This tiny town consisted of a handful of houses, a railroad station, and a few shops and businesses. It was easy for the robbers to round up virtually the entire population of the town and hold them captive in the station, preventing them from riding off and sounding an alarm.

The gang tore out the town's telegraph equipment (despite the protests of the ignorant Bassham, who thought it was a sewing machine). They piled timber and debris on the track and put out the signal to stop the train. As the train slowed, the robbers jumped onboard, but the gang was disappointed. They had expected a shipment of gold worth $380,000. Instead, their haul was later estimated to be $6,000 to $35,000.

After the robbery, the prisoners were released and the train was allowed to continue. The bandits fled, but not before Jesse left one of his characteristic notes for publication: "We are the boys who are hard to handle, and we will make it hot for the party that ever tries to take us."

GROWING MISTRUST

As usual, Jesse was not active over the winter, but he resumed his life of crime in 1880. One job was the holdup of a tourist coach at Mammoth Cave, in an isolated part of central Kentucky. In another caper, the gang robbed a store in Mercer, Kentucky. The outlaws had hoped (but failed) to find a large payroll that was destined for miners working nearby.

Meanwhile, the gang's leader was having trouble with his new band's members. They were young and untested. They were also constantly fighting with one another, usually over money or women. Furthermore, he believed they were untrustworthy. Jesse became suspicious of their motives, suspecting that one or another intended to betray him. The amateurism and mistrust among the group was in sharp contrast to the James-Younger Gang, which had consisted of loyal, hard-bitten ex-bushwhackers and former soldiers.

CHANGING MEMBERSHIP, CHANGING FORTUNES

Despite his intentions, Frank was apparently unable to give up the outlaw life completely. There is evidence that he was an occasional member of the new band, probably at his brother's request. Carl W. Breihan notes, "Without Jesse's initiatives, Frank James would have dropped into less hazardous ways."

The membership of the gang was constantly changing as men continuously joined and left the group. In a statement Liddil later made to authorities, he asserted, "There were in all during its whole career twenty one men in this band. As a man [left] another man was recruited, until its final downfall."

Some were captured. One of these was the Jameses' cousin, Clarence Hite. Others were murdered, including another cousin, Wood Hite, who was probably killed by two other gang members. They had argued over the division of money from a robbery in Blue Cut, Missouri, in September 1881.

A few simply vanished, like Ed Miller, and still others fled, such as Dick Liddil, who grew frightened of Jesse's growing mistrust and paranoia. Fearing he would be killed, Liddil made a deal with the authorities. He agreed to reveal what he knew about the James Gang in exchange for immunity from prosecution.

As the band increasingly slid into disarray, Jesse's fortunes changed in other ways, as well. One aspect of this was that the public's interest in him was waning; the emotions of the Civil War were fading and the appeal of revenge against the North was also receding. Furthermore, it was increasingly obvious that the James Gang

Jesse James's popularity among the public began to wane as the years progressed. People began to see Jesse and the gang not as Robin Hoods but as common criminals. Thomas Crittenden, a former Union colonel and the governor of Missouri, offered a reward for the capture of Jesse, dead or alive.

was primarily interested in profit, not in upholding Southern ideals or helping the poor. As a result, the public was far less sympathetic than it had once been. People increasingly felt that the outlaws were just criminals, not folk heroes.

Even those who had once been staunch supporters now felt otherwise. T.J. Stiles writes, "Jesse and his comrades had symbolized secessionist resentments, but [now] there was nothing left to resent."

NO SYMPATHY

Politicians like Missouri governor Thomas Crittenden were also becoming less tolerant of outlaws, especially the James Gang. Crittenden made this clear in his inaugural address when he declared that he had "a solemn determination to overthrow and to destroy outlawry in this state whose head and front is the James gang."

By law, Crittenden could not offer a large government-sponsored reward for Jesse's capture. A reward such as this would have been tempting enough to risk the danger of turning Jesse in.

Crittenden, however, was able to successfully persuade railroad and express companies to offer a total of $10,000 in bounties for each of the James brothers and $5,000 for other gang members. Crittenden announced that the public should "[r]ise en masse, by day or night, until the entire band is either captured or exterminated."

Besides politicians and the public, newspapers were growing less sympathetic toward crime. The *Chicago Times* called Missouri "The Outlaw's Paradise," and the city's other newspaper, *Inter-Ocean*, wrote, "In no State but Missouri would the James brothers be tolerated for twelve years." Even James's once loyal supporter, John Newman Edwards, essentially ended the publicity campaign that had made the outlaw famous.

MOVING AROUND

Meanwhile, it was increasingly difficult for Jesse to maintain anonymity in Tennessee. Fearing discovery by neighbors, he moved his family to Kansas City, Missouri, in 1881. Frank also moved back to Missouri for a time but left for Virginia, hoping to permanently lead a quiet life.

Jesse kept the name Thomas Howard and also grew a beard, which he dyed black. His new identity was so effective that not even his children knew his real name. They thought the family name was Howard.

The outlaw stayed in Kansas City only a short time before moving to another Missouri town, St. Joseph. The family rented a succession of houses there. The last of these was a neat little home, white with green trim, at 1318 Lafayette Street.

As usual, Jesse was rarely home. He was often off on a raid, frequently staying with relatives or friends. But even this became increasingly difficult, as James had to rely on threats and intimidation, not on friendship or sympathy, to get shelter. Many felt he deserved death. A neighbor, Bettie Scruggs Patton, wrote to a friend, "Anybody that knows anything about Jesse, knows that whenever he's captured, a black box will suit him better than chains."

When at home, however, Jesse was a different man and a regular citizen of "St. Joe." He liked to spend time in a drugstore where he bought cigars and chatted amiably. According to one story, he even boldly applied for a job at the railroad depot, asserting that he had extensive experience in the express business.

A MURDER PLOT DEVELOPS

Once his brother permanently retired from the gang, Jesse James came to believe that only two members of the group could be trusted. Jesse's mother allegedly warned him against trusting anyone too much, but the bandit had confidence in his instincts.

The two men he trusted were Bob and Charley Ford. Charley had already taken part in several of the gang's robberies, but as of 1882 his younger brother Bob was a relatively new recruit.

Despite James's instincts, the Fords were indeed untrustworthy. They were greedy for reward money and eager for the fame they believed would come from killing the famous outlaw. They also had another reason to betray their boss: Bob was worried about being charged with the earlier murder of Wood Hite. He hoped that by killing Jesse James he would avoid prosecution for it.

THE FORD BROTHERS' CHANCE

It is not certain if the Fords initially made contact with the authorities or vice versa. It is known, however, that Bob traveled at least twice to Kansas City to talk to Crittenden in secret. The brothers also apparently spoke with J.R. Timberlake, the sheriff of Clay County, about betraying their infamous boss.

On April 1, 1882, Jesse rode to the home of Elias Ford, a relative of the Ford brothers, in Ray County. Bob and Charley were staying there. He told Bob that he had work planned for him and his brother—a bank robbery in Platte City, Missouri, on April 4.

Jesse and Charley rode back together to St. Joseph. The next day, Elias Ford notified Sheriff Timberlake of this turn of events. Bob soon joined the others at the James house, and the sheriff told his posse to stand ready.

On the morning of April 3, after breakfast at the James home, the three bandits began to prepare their horses and equipment. It was a warm day, and Jesse removed his coat and guns. Some historians have wondered why he did this, because it was unusual for the robber to go unarmed at any time. There is even speculation that he may have done it deliberately, because he wanted to die.

"I HAVE KILLED JESSE JAMES"

The Fords knew that the only way to kill Jesse James was to catch him unarmed. This was their chance. Charley later stated, "I knew he was quicker than I, and [he] was so watchful that no man could get the drop on him."

With his gang down to just a few members, Jesse thought that the only people he could trust were the Ford brothers, Bob (*pictured, with the gun he used to kill Jesse James*) and Charley. Only 20 years old, Bob was an eager recruit. For his involvement in the murder of Jesse's cousin Wood Hite, Bob was offered a pardon and the reward money if he would kill Jesse.

The fateful moment came when Jesse noticed something wrong with a picture on the wall. In one version of the story, it was crooked; in another it needed dusting. In either case, James stood on a chair, turning his back to the Fords.

Some accounts assert that Charley was in the next room and that only Bob fired when Jesse's back was turned. Wherever Charley was, Bob Ford succeeded in shooting Jesse James in the head.

On hearing the gunfire, Zee ran in. The Fords later testified that she screamed in grief but that overall she took in the terrible situation with surprising calm. Perhaps she had been anticipating such a moment for years.

The Fords ran out of the house and went straight to the telegraph office to alert Crittenden and Timberlake. The message read: "I HAVE KILLED JESSE JAMES. ST. JOSEPH. BOB FORD."

HE DIED WITH HIS BOOTS ON

By the time the killers returned to the James house, a crowd had gathered. They were astonished to realize that the genial neighbor they knew as Mr. Howard was, in fact, the world's most famous outlaw. One reporter commented, "Those who were standing near drew in their breaths at the thought of being so near Jesse James, even if he was dead."

The town marshal, Enos Craig, was also there. The Ford brothers identified themselves and demanded their reward, but Craig temporarily put them in jail. During this period the sheriff's young son, Corydon, befriended the Fords and supplied them with cigarettes and good food. On his release, Bob Ford presented Corydon with the murder weapon, a Smith & Wesson .44. (The bullet that killed Jesse remained in the coroner's family for many years.)

News about the robber's death spread quickly. The headline in the St. Joseph *Evening News* was typical. It read, "JUDGMENT FOR JESSE—THE NOTORIOUS BANDIT AT LAST MEETS HIS FATE AND DIES WITH HIS BOOTS ON."

IDENTIFYING THE BODY

Jesse's body was taken to the local funeral home for an autopsy. It was confirmed that the bullet entered behind his right ear, angled upward, and emerged near the left temple. The autopsy also

The Bandit's Body

The St. Joseph coroner positively identified the body shot by Robert Ford as that of Jesse James. In addition, four people who knew the bandit—a former bushwhacker, a friend, a neighbor, and Dick Liddil's wife—testified that the identification was correct. They wrote:

St. Joseph, Mo., April 4, 1882.

We, the undersigned, hereby certify that we were well acquainted with Jesse James during his lifetime, that we have just viewed his remains now in the custody of the coroner at this place and have no hesitation in saying that they are unquestionably his.

Harrison Trow

William J. Clay

James Wilkerson

Mattie Liddil

revealed that Jesse's brain was larger than average, although both it and the skull were "dreadfully shattered."

After the autopsy, one of the authorities' tasks was to certify that the body was indeed that of Jesse James. Since few photographs of him existed, this was not an easy task. There was, however, a good deal of evidence. For example, the body had two large bullet-wound scars on the right side of the chest and another in one leg. Also, the left middle finger was missing its tip. These injuries were consistent with wounds Jesse James had received.

Investigators further found one of James's known birth-marks, a large brown spot on the back of his right arm. In addition, there was evidence of an injured left ankle that had never healed properly, consistent with the damage the bandit suffered during the Gallatin robbery. Other physical characteristics matched as well. For example, the body was five feet nine or ten (175 to 178 centimeters), slender and compactly built, with a size-32 waist.

All of this evidence was enough to conclude that the body was that of the outlaw. The coroner's jury noted, "We the jury find that the deceased is Jesse James, and that he came to his death from a pistol in the hands of Robert Ford."

TRAITOR! TRAITOR!

Following the autopsy came a formal inquest at the St. Joseph courthouse. For the next two days, six citizens heard testimony about the murder, including statements from the Ford brothers. After arguing that they were afraid of attack by the public, the Fords were allowed to remain armed in the courthouse.

Bob Ford testified, "Governor Crittenden had offered a $10,000 reward for Jesse, dead or alive. We knew that the only way was to kill him. He was always cool and self-possessed, and always on the watch." He also testified that both Fords had drawn their weapons. This differed from the story he had first told reporters: that Charley was in the next room when the shot was fired.

Zee James also testified at the inquest. Her statement included the admission that "Thomas Howard" was really Jesse James. She further stated that he had been an affectionate father and a thoughtful, loving husband.

Zerelda James and Dick Liddil were also in attendance. Jesse's mother apparently believed that Liddil was involved in her son's murder. According to writer William A. Settle Jr., as she left the room, Zerelda pointed a finger at Liddil and shouted, "Traitor! Traitor! Traitor! God will send vengeance on you for this; you are the cause of all this. Oh, you villain; I would rather be in my boy's place than in yours!"

The murder of Jesse James was a national phenomenon. While the Ford brothers went to claim their reward, crowds pressed into Jesse's small home in St. Joseph to see his body. Despite rumors that Frank would avenge his brother Jesse's death at the funeral, large crowds continued to attend the formal viewing at the Kearney Hotel.

REPORTING THE STORY

The Missouri press covered the murder and its aftermath extensively. The news spread and, like so much about Jesse James, made headlines nationwide. Reporters contacted relatives, neighbors, former bushwhackers, and anyone else who could tell their (often fanciful) stories about Jesse and his comrades.

Despite their period of estrangement, John Newman Edwards was Jesse James's most vocal and sympathetic mourner. Writing in the Sedalia (Missouri) *Democrat*, Edwards commented, "We called him outlaw, and he was; but fate made him so." He also compared the outlaw to another famous victim of assassination, Julius Caesar, and the killers to a betrayer from the Bible: "Indignation . . . is . . . thundering over the land that if a single one of the miserable assassins had either manhood, conscience, or courage, he would go, as another Judas, and hang himself."

The undertaker's note in the ledger of his funeral home was much less flowery. It read: "Apr. 3 Mr. Jesse James killed. Number 11 S. [State] casket with shroud, $250. Shroud $10 paid." It was rumored at the time that Timberlake and Craig, the sheriff and marshal who had been key in the murder plot, covered the funeral costs.

THE FUNERAL

Strangers flocked to the funeral home to see the body. As they arrived, there were rumors that Frank would come to avenge his brother's death, but he never appeared. When Jesse's body was released, Zee and Zerelda accompanied it on the train to Kearney. Some 2,000 people—the largest crowd ever seen in the bandit's hometown—came to view the body at the Kearney Hotel.

After a memorial service at Mount Olivet Baptist Church, a funeral procession went to the family home. The body of the outlaw was buried there, beneath a large tree. Zerelda wrote the epitaph for the gravestone:

In Loving Remembrance of My Beloved Son,
JESSE W. JAMES.
Died April 3, 1882.
Aged 34 Years, 6 Months, 28 Days.
Murdered by a Traitor and Coward whose
Name is Not Worthy to Appear Here.

Jesse's stepfather, Dr. Reuben Samuel, told reporters that flower seeds soon arrived at the farm from all over the country. Notes accompanying them said that they were meant to decorate Jesse's grave. According to Samuel, there were enough seeds to blanket his entire farm.

THE AFTERMATH
OF THE MURDER

As Jesse James's funeral arrangements and burial were taking place, the Ford brothers formally surrendered to authorities. They had expected to be congratulated. To their surprise, they were promptly put in jail and charged with first-degree murder.

The brothers were tried and sentenced to die by hanging. Governor Thomas Crittenden, however, pardoned the Fords only two hours after their conviction. His stated reason was that they deserved to go free because they had rid the state of a notorious criminal.

THE OUTLAWS WERE WELL KNOWN

Many people considered the pardon suspicious. It suggested that Crittenden had been aware all along that the brothers intended to kill Jesse James and that he unofficially approved of it. The implication that the chief executive of Missouri may have conspired to kill a private citizen shocked and outraged much of the public.

On the other hand, many people and newspaper writers expressed relief that James was dead and considered the Fords to have done a good deed. For instance, an editorial in the New York *Illustrated Times* commented:

> The outlaws were well known; yet they robbed, wrecked, plundered and assassinated with impunity. The injury which the Jesse James gang inflicted upon Missouri is beyond calculation. . . . No man ventured within its borders unless the stern necessities of business compelled him. When a traveler got into a Missouri train he did so with the same feeling that a man has when going into battle—with little expectation of getting through alive.

THE FATE OF THE FORDS

The Ford brothers had hoped to be rewarded well. Instead, they received only a small portion of the promised $10,000. The bulk went to various law-enforcement officials who had taken part in the scheme to kill James.

The Fords did not have happy lives in the years after their dramatic deed. Their neighbors regarded the brothers with hostility, and life in Missouri became intolerable for them. Charley, deeply depressed, contracted tuberculosis and committed suicide in Richmond, Missouri, in 1884, just two years after the murder.

Bob went on tour with a traveling theatrical show that reenacted the James murder. The famous promoter P.T. Barnum also hired Bob for a time to be in his show of curiosities. Neither of these ventures lasted long.

After years of heavy drinking and gambling, Bob Ford was killed in a barroom fight in 1892. His death occurred in the saloon he ran in the boomtown of Creede, Colorado. Bob was not generally mourned. Carl W. Breihan comments, "Popular opinion reached the verdict that Robert Ford was the most contemptible coward ever to go unhanged."

Throughout their lives, Zerelda James Samuel continued to support Jesse and Frank, declaring that "No mother ever had better sons." She portrayed her family as innocent victims of government authorities. After the murder of Jesse, Zerelda sold pebbles from his gravesite for a quarter each.

SIGHTSEERS

As she had all along, Zerelda Samuel fiercely defended her sons' reputations in the years after the murder. She told reporters over and over that Frank and Jesse were the best sons any mother could have and that they had been cruelly wronged. For the most part, until her death in Oklahoma City in 1911, she resisted efforts to make money by trading on their fame. At one point, she allegedly refused an offer of $10,000 for Jesse's body from a promoter who wanted to display it publicly.

Zerelda, however, was not above charging visitors a little money to view the house and Jesse's grave. She charged more if people wanted to take a pebble from the grave as a souvenir. The supply of pebbles never seemed to end—it was regularly replenished from a nearby riverbed.

Meanwhile, the owner of Jesse James's last home in St. Joseph, where the murder took place, charged sightseers to tour it. These visitors were not shy about taking mementos. William A. Settle Jr. comments that the dime admittance fee was "a modest amount, in view of the fact that the fence and stables were almost demolished by relic hunters who carried away splinters of wood from the structures as souvenirs."

FRANK SURRENDERS

Frank, still living elsewhere, decided to surrender about half a year after Jesse's murder. In a deal brokered by the James boys' old supporter, John Newman Edwards, Frank met with Governor Crittenden in Jefferson City, the capital of Missouri.

After Frank surrendered, he was taken to Independence, Missouri. Settle writes, "News of the surrender had covered the state, and as [his] train progressed toward Independence, people along the way thronged to the stations for a glance at Frank James. . . . [H]undreds were on hand to witness his arrival at Independence where his wife, mother, and small son greeted him."

Crittenden had agreed to keep the former outlaw from extradition to any other state. Specifically, he would not be sent to Minnesota for prosecution stemming from the Northfield raid. In return, Frank agreed to keep a low profile after standing trial for two of his crimes: the Gallatin robbery and murders and the 1881 robbery of an Army Corps of Engineers payroll in Alabama.

During the trial for the Gallatin case, the outlaw was portrayed as a war hero because of his guerrilla activities. It was also demonstrated that he had tried to maintain a normal life for many years. The jury was sympathetic, and Frank was acquitted. He was later acquitted in the Alabama case, too. A writer for the Sedalia (Missouri)

Having been acquitted of his crimes, Frank James retired and worked in a variety of jobs such as shoe salesman, telegraph operator, and theater guard. He enjoyed a quiet life on the James family farm with his wife and son Robert, giving tours for a quarter, until his death in 1915 at age 72.

Daily Democrat spoke for many when he commented, "It is time to draw the veil of charity over the terrible past, and to deal honorably and fairly with Frank James."

FRANK'S LAST YEARS

Frank James lived for another three decades. During this time he held a number of jobs, including shoe salesman, telegraph operator, betting commissioner, doorman, livestock trader, and theater guard. For a period after Cole Younger's parole in 1901, the two created a traveling show. Their program was called "The Great Cole Younger and Frank James Historical Wild West Show."

Zerelda willed the family farm to her surviving son. After her death Frank enjoyed a quiet life there with his wife, Anne, and their son, Robert Franklin, occasionally giving tours of the farm. Frank James died in 1915, age 72, and was buried in Independence.

Frank was often remembered in a positive light. People re-called his relative gentleness, reserve, and scholarly nature, partic-ularly his love of Shakespeare and the theater. William Pinkerton, the son of the detective agency's founder, later told a St. Louis newspaper, "I rather like Frank James. It is my impression that his brother Jesse was the vindictive and cruel one of the two. If it hadn't been for Jesse, I am inclined to think Frank would have become a good citizen long before he did."

Not everyone agreed. The Atchison (Kansas) *Champion* com-mented, "Jesse James was hunted and killed just as he should have been hunted and killed, and if his scarcely less vicious and criminal brother wants to escape the just penalty of his many cruel deeds, let him go to Mexico, or South America, or anywhere else out of this country, in which he has no right to live."

ZEE AND HER CHILDREN

As for Jesse's wife, Zee, life was difficult after her husband's death. She was pregnant when her husband was killed, but she had a mis-carriage. Meanwhile, her financial situation became increasingly desperate.

Many items found in the James home matched those stolen in various robberies, and these were returned to their owners. Left with only a few possessions, Zee was forced to sell many of them for cash to satisfy creditors. Even Jesse Jr.'s little dog, Boo, was sold for $5. Efforts by her church and others to raise money for the widow were unsuccessful.

Zee's money troubles were connected to rumors of the James brothers having hidden vast amounts of money around the state. These rumors were apparently false. It is reasonable to assume that, if this money existed, Frank would have been able to help her.

The widow and her children relocated to Kansas City. Despite needing cash, Zee never agreed to write books or otherwise trade on her husband's notoriety. Depressed, grief-stricken, and impoverished, Zee died in 1900. She was buried in the Mount Olivet Cemetery in Kearney. In 1902, in accordance with Zee's wishes, her husband's remains were moved next to hers. Jesse's mother and stepfather are also buried there.

Jesse James Jr., who was seven when his father died, went to work at an early age. He later became a respected lawyer in Kansas City and Los Angeles, and died in Los Angeles in 1951. He and his sister, Mary, appeared in two 1921 silent movies about their famous father. Mary wed Henry Lafayette Barr in 1901, had four children, and died in 1935 in Kansas City.

RUMORS OF A FAKED DEATH

As Frank settled into a quiet life, rumors about his notorious brother's death swirled, including stories that he had not died. For example, it was widely rumored that Robert Ford had actually killed a James look-alike—perhaps Charles Bigelow, who was briefly in the outlaw's gang. Jesse allegedly attended his own funeral before leaving for South America.

Such rumors have never been proven. An attempt was made in 1995 to settle the question. The body in Jesse James's grave was exhumed and subjected to DNA analysis. The results were inconclusive, stating only that the remains were consistent with the DNA of the James family.

Meanwhile, in the years after Jesse James's death, some dozen imposters came forward claiming to be the outlaw. Prominent among these was J. Frank Dalton, a native Texan who in 1948 asserted that he was Jesse James.

Dalton's story was suspicious. For starters, prior to his announcement that he was Jesse, he had claimed to be Frank Dalton, a well-known deputy U.S. marshal in the Oklahoma Territory and the brother of the Dalton brothers, who formed a notorious group of robbers called the Dalton Gang. Nonetheless, Dalton maintained his assertion about being Jesse James, receiving widespread publicity until his death in 1951, aged about 103.

Frank's son, Robert, pointed out that not a single imposter who came forward had any definite identifying marks on his body. Robert James commented, "I have had eleven Uncle Jesses. . . . They bob up every once in a while. None of them has ever come to see me, though. They are too busy at fairs, rodeos, and making money out of it. At one time two of them were operating at the same time. So far none has had the missing fingertip."

THAT DIRTY LITTLE COWARD

While he was alive, Jesse James was a hero mostly to former Confederates and even to some Northerners (especially boys) who were thrilled to read the dime novels written about him. His popularity continued to grow among the general public after his demise. Breihan writes, "Although many a robber . . . has passed over the land since the days of Jesse James, he is the outlaw whose feats seem destined to be remembered longest."

In the years after his death, a number of popular ballads sprang up about him. Probably the best known (although it was incorrect about the number of James's children) began:

Jesse James was a lad that killed many a man,
He robbed the Danville train.
But that dirty little coward that shot Mr. Howard
Has laid poor Jesse in his grave.

Poor Jesse had a wife to mourn for his life,
Three children, they were brave,
But the dirty little coward that shot Mr. Howard
Has laid poor Jesse in his grave.

In the years since, James's fame has spread worldwide and continues to endure. Many people still find him a fascinating and even admirable figure. For example, one of Missouri's most famous natives, U.S. president Harry S. Truman, commented, "Jesse James was not actually a bad man at heart. . . . I am convinced that Jesse would have been an asset to his community, if he had not been diverted into a lawless life."

REMEMBERING JESSE JAMES

After Frank's death, his son Robert inherited the family farm. Robert then passed it on to his second wife, May. She lived there until her death in 1974. The property lay in disrepair for some years afterward, until the Clay County Parks Department bought the place and restored it as a museum. Among the artifacts visitors can see there are Jesse's last pair of boots, his last cartridge belt and bridle, and the feather duster he allegedly was holding when he was murdered.

Meanwhile, the house in St. Joseph where Jesse was killed has also been made into a museum. Visitors can see such memorabilia as the handles from the outlaw's coffin, a tiepin he wore on the day of his death, a bullet removed from near his right lung, and a casting of his skull, showing the wound that killed him. Both the bank that was the scene of the Northfield raid and the funeral home where Jesse's body was taken have displays about him as well.

A number of annual events honor and maintain the memory of the bandit. Among them are the Defeat of Jesse James Days in Northfield, Minnesota; the Jesse James Festival in his home town of Kearney; and the Jesse James International Arts and Film Festival in Russellville, Kentucky. Furthermore, Russellville's Tobacco and Heritage Festival features a five-kilometer race named for James and a re-enactment of his raid on the town's bank.

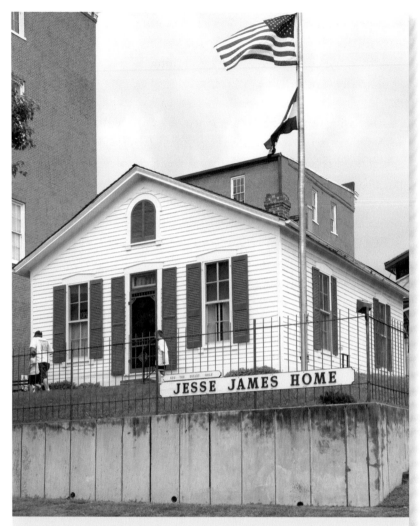

The Jesse James Home Museum in St. Joseph, Missouri, is the place where the outlaw lived and was gunned down in 1882. The bullet hole in the wall is still intact (though now larger due to tourists carving into it) and the house contains a number of items owned by the James family. The home is listed on the National Register of Historic Places.

Jesse James's life has also been extensively considered in books, particularly the (largely invented) dime novels celebrating the outlaw's exploits. Novels and nonfiction books about him have numbered in the hundreds. Most are now out of print, and writer Richard E. Meyer comments, "[I]n a vast majority of instances this might be considered a very good thing, as few among them contain anything of value to the general reader."

Jesse's story has also been told in at least 75 movies or television shows, dating back to the 1920s silent movies his children appeared in. Notable among these is *The Long Riders* (which featured three sets of real-life brothers as the Jameses, Youngers, and Fords). More recently, Brad Pitt, Sam Shepard, and Casey Affleck appeared as, respectively, Jesse James, Frank James, and Bob Ford in *The Assassination of Jesse James by the Coward Robert Ford*.

During his lifetime, the famous outlaw fascinated people, and that fascination continues to this day. William A. Settle Jr. comments, "Even today, even in the remotest way, the James story arouses attention." No doubt the outlaw's fame will continue for years to come. Meyer adds, "Perhaps no period in American history has created so many folk rebels. . . . And amongst them all one name, more recognizable to most Americans than the majority of their past presidents, stands supreme: Jesse James."

CHRONOLOGY

1847   Jesse James is born on September 5 in Clay County, Missouri.

1861   The American Civil War breaks out.

1863 or 1864   Jesse joins his first group of bushwhackers (pro-South guerrilla fighters) in Missouri, then joins William T. "Bloody Bill" Anderson's gang.

TIMELINE

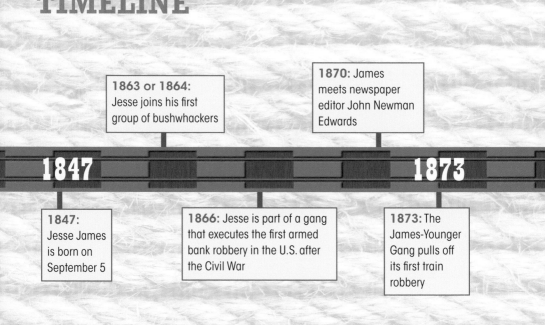

1863 or 1864: Jesse joins his first group of bushwhackers

1870: James meets newspaper editor John Newman Edwards

1847

1873

1847: Jesse James is born on September 5

1866: Jesse is part of a gang that executes the first armed bank robbery in the U.S. after the Civil War

1873: The James-Younger Gang pulls off its first train robbery

1865–1866   After he suffers a serious gunshot to a lung, James is nursed back to health by his cousin Zee.

1866   A gang of former bushwhackers led by Archie Clement and including Frank and Jesse James executes the first armed bank robbery in the United States after the war. The gang continues to rob a succession of banks. When Clement is killed, the James brothers keep the band of robbers going, forming the basis for the James-Younger Gang.

1870   James meets newspaper editor John Newman Edwards, who plays a key role in making the outlaw famous.

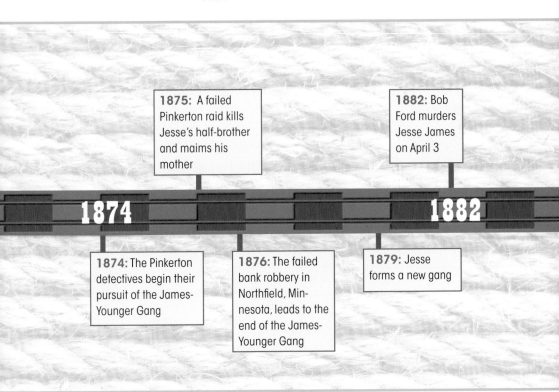

1875: A failed Pinkerton raid kills Jesse's half-brother and maims his mother

1882: Bob Ford murders Jesse James on April 3

1874   **1882**

1874: The Pinkerton detectives begin their pursuit of the James-Younger Gang

1876: The failed bank robbery in Northfield, Minnesota, leads to the end of the James-Younger Gang

1879: Jesse forms a new gang

1873 The James-Younger Gang pulls off its first train robbery, near Adair, Iowa.

1874 The Pinkertons, agents of the National Detective Agency, begin their pursuit of the outlaws. Cousins Zee Mimms and Jesse James marry.

1875 Son Jesse James Jr. is born. A failed Pinkerton raid kills Frank and Jesse's half-brother and maims their mother. Jesse moves his family to Tennessee, and they adopt new identities.

1876 A robbery attempt of the bank in Northfield, Minnesota, fails disastrously and effectively ends the James-Younger Gang.

1879 Daughter Mary James is born. Jesse forms a new gang.

1881 James moves his family back to Missouri as their ability to maintain anonymity in Tennessee diminishes.

1882 Jesse James is murdered on April 3 at his house in St. Joseph, Missouri, by Bob Ford, a member of his gang who hoped to collect a reward.

GLOSSARY

abolish To ban. People who opposed slavery were called "abolitionists."

amnesty A pardon for a crime. Someone who receives amnesty cannot be prosecuted for that crime.

autopsy The medical examination of a corpse to determine the cause of death.

bushwhackers Pro-Southern guerrilla fighters during the Civil War.

combustible Explosive or ready to explode.

exhume Dig up from the ground. Buried bodies are sometimes exhumed for scientific reasons, such as DNA analysis to prove identity.

extradition The handing over of an alleged criminal from one jurisdiction (a state or a country) to another to stand trial.

guerrilla A member of a small group of combatants, not regular military. Guerrillas typically carry out small-scale surprise raids on the enemy.

incendiary Burnable or ready to burn.

inquest A legal inquiry into the details of a crime or an event.

jayhawkers The nickname of antislavery guerrilla fighters from Kansas, who often crossed the border to raid the slave state of Missouri.

lynchings   Murders committed for racial reasons, often by hanging or burning.

massacre   The killing of a large group of unarmed soldiers or civilians.

paranoia   A mental state that causes the sufferer to believe irrationally that everyone is out to do him or her harm.

posse   In the Old West, a group of lawmen or private citizens who assembled to chase an outlaw, typically on horseback.

prairie chicken   A large bird, similar to a grouse.

reconstruction   The name given to the period after the Civil War when the South required rebuilding, both literally (in the form of repairing or rebuilding destroyed property) and figuratively (in the form of creating new laws, forms of government, social programs, etc.).

secede   To break away from an established organization or country and form a new one. The Civil War broke out after Southern states seceded from the United States to form the Confederate States of America.

tuberculosis   A serious respiratory illness.

BIBLIOGRAPHY

Breihan, Carl W. *Saga of Jesse James*. Caldwell, Idaho: Caxton Press, 1991.

———. *The Day Jesse James Was Killed*. New York: Fell, 1961.

Bruns, Roger A. *The Bandit Kings: From Jesse James to Pretty Boy Floyd*. New York: Crown, 1995.

Croy, Homer. *Jesse James Was My Neighbor*. Lincoln, Neb.: University of Nebraska Press, 1997.

Horan, James D. *Desperate Men: The James Gang and the Wild Bunch*. Lincoln, Neb.: University of Nebraska Press, 1997.

James, Jesse Jr. "Outlawed and Hunted," *Jesse James My Father*. Available online. URL: http://www.civilwarstlouis.com/History/jamesgangjessejr8.htm.

Miller, George W. Jr. *The Trial of Frank James for Murder, with Confessions of Dick Liddil and Clarence Hite*. New York: Jingle Bob/Crown, 1977.

"Old West Songs: Jesse James," Teddy Blue's Bunkhouse. Available online. URL: http://www.wildwestweb.net/jessejames.html.

Settle, William A. Jr. *Jesse James Was His Name*. Columbia, Mo.: University of Missouri Press, 1966.

Smith, Robert Barr. *The Last Hurrah of the James-Younger Gang*. Norman, Okla.: University of Oklahoma Press, 2001.

Stewart, Phil. "The Plot to Capture Jesse James," Stray Leaves: Jesse James Contents. Available online. URL: http://www.ericjames.org/Meet_Phil_Stewart.html/.

Stiles, T.J. *Jesse James: Last Rebel of the Civil War*. New York: Vintage, 2003.

FURTHER RESOURCES

Brant, Marley. *Jesse James: The Man and the Myth*. New York: Berkley Trade, 1998.

———. *The Outlaw Youngers: A Confederate Brotherhood*. Lanham, Md.: Madison Books, 1995.

Castel, Albert, and Thomas Goodrich. *Bloody Bill Anderson: The Short, Savage Life of a Civil War Guerrilla*. Mechanicsburg, Pa.: Stackpole Books, 1998.

Dellinger, Harold. *Jesse James: The Best Writing on the Notorious Outlaw and His Gang*. Guilford, Conn.: Globe Pequot, 2007.

Yeatman, Ted P. *Frank and Jesse James: The Story Behind the Legend*. Nashville, Tenn.: Cumberland House Publishing, 2000.

DVDs

Indigo Films (producer). *Jesse James: American Outlaw*. San Francisco: Indigo Films, 2006.

Andrew Dominik (director). *The Assassination of Jesse James by the Coward Robert Ford*. Warner Brothers, 2007. An excellent and quite accurate film starring Brad Pitt and Sam Shepard as Jesse and Frank James.

Walter Hill (director). *The Long Riders*. MGM Studios, 1980. A beautifully filmed story notable for using actors who are real-life sets of brothers as the Jameses, the Youngers, and the Fords.

Philip Kaufman (director). *The Great Northfield Minnesota Raid*. Universal Studios, 1972. This is an entertaining but not very accurate retelling of the legendary last robbery, starring Robert Duvall as Jesse James and Cliff Robertson as Cole Younger.

Web Sites

American Experience: Jesse James

http://www.pbs.org/wgbh/amex/james/

A Web site based on the 2006 PBS program.

Dime Novels—Jesse James, the Outlaw

http://www-sul.stanford.edu/depts/dp/pennies/texts/lawson_toc.html

This site, maintained by Stanford University, reproduces the cover and text of a 1901 "dime novel" about the robber.

Jesse James—Folklore Hero or Cold-Blooded Killer?

http://www.legendsofamerica.com/WE-JesseJames.html

Part of "Legends of America," a site devoted to American history.

PICTURE CREDITS

Page

INDEX

121

ABOUT THE AUTHOR

Adam Woog has written more than 60 books for adults, young adults, and children. He is especially interested in history and biography. Woog lives in his hometown of Seattle, Washington, with his wife and their daughter.